Sienna's Story

Sienna's Story

THE BIOGRAPHY OF BRITAIN'S MOST INSPIRING STAR

Sarah Marshall

JOHN BLAKE

Published by John Blake Publishing Ltd,
3 Bramber Court, 2 Bramber Road,
London W14 9PB, England

www.blake.co.uk

First published in hardback in 2006

ISBN-10: 1 84454 296 3
ISBN-13: 978 1 84454 295 6

British Library Cataloguing-in-Publication Data:

A catalogue record for this book is available from the British Library.

Design by www.envydesign.co.uk

Printed and bound in Great Britain by William Clowes Ltd, Beccles, Suffolk

1 3 5 7 9 10 8 6 4 2

Papers used by John Blake Publishing are natural, recyclable products made from wood grown in sustainable forests. The manufacturing processes conform to the environmental regulations of the country of origin.

Every attempt has been made to contact the relevant copyright-holders, but some were unobtainable. We would be grateful if the appropriate people could contact us.

With love to Mum, for your support
and enduring patience.

Contents

ONE

The Sugar Plum Fairy

CRYSTALLINE snowflakes started to settle on the windscreen of the beaten-up New York cab that Josephine Miller had hailed only five minutes earlier. Despite the whirs and splutters of an engine in desperate need of attention, she'd hardly moved five metres in that time. Leaning forward, she tried to gauge exactly what the problem could be. Aside from the odd motorcyclist weaving past wing mirrors at breakneck speed, the traffic ahead was gridlocked. Frustratingly, her driver was refusing to switch on the windscreen wipers and, beyond a sea of canary-coloured alloy, her vision blurred into infinity. Squinting through a watery veil of partially melted ice, she tried to figure out how much further it was to the theatre.

If her so-called streetwise cabbie didn't put his foot down, she was going to miss the show.

'Excuse me,' said Josephine, tapping on the driver's window. 'Exactly what seems to be the problem?'

No reply. Humming away to a song on the radio, he seemed to be oblivious to his passenger.

'Excuse me!' she shouted, now at twice the volume. Noticing the driver was now shifting his seat, she felt triumphant at having elicited a response.

'What's the problem, lady?' he drawled nonchalantly, all the while chewing loudly on a piece of gum.

'I'm going to be late for my show. Can't we take a shortcut?' she said with a sigh, now tugging nervously at her watch strap. It was only 15 minutes until curtain call and Ed would be waiting for her. For weeks, she'd been dying to see George Balanchine's adaptation of *The Nutcracker* for the City Ballet and was over the moon when he had presented her with two tickets as a last-minute stocking filler. If only she'd kept a proper eye on the time, she wouldn't be running late now.

'Sorry, lady. Nothing I can do,' replied the driver, with a shrug. 'Mid-town, early evening traffic. All these people sick of sitting at home with the family. That's Manhattan for you!'

Slumping back in her seat, Josephine wondered what to do. Outside the sidewalks were strewn with human balls of fur, hurriedly scuttling towards their destinations. Judging by the quality of haute-couture clothing, the New York State Theater couldn't be too far away.

'Forget it,' smiled Josephine at the driver through clenched teeth. 'I'll walk.' Fortunately, she'd been right to trust her instincts. Within a matter of minutes she was on a direct course for the theatre. Walking at a pace, she felt relieved to be wearing a pair of flats. Only two blocks to go! she thought, now elated. But only three minutes 'til showtime.

Inside the theatre foyer, flustered staff were desperately trying to usher latecomers to their seats. 'Where have you been?' cried Ed, visibly concerned by his wife's uncharacteristic tardiness. 'You didn't walk here, did you?' he went on, narrowing his gaze to focus on the mound of white flakes collecting like a ruff around her neck.

'The traffic was terrible!' she protested, hurriedly slipping out of her damp overcoat. 'I had no choice but to walk.'

'For goodness sake, Josephine!' Ed chastised her. 'It's minus three degrees out there and you're nine months pregnant!'

She mumbled a reply, knowing full well her usually overprotective husband was on this occasion unusually right. Then, quickly switching subjects in an attempt to avoid an argument, she said, 'Circle or stalls?'

As Josephine had expected, the performance was exemplary. There was something so delicate, magical and ethereal about *The Nutcracker*. No other story could capture the Christmas spirit quite so perfectly. After Tchaikovsky had composed the ballet score in the late 19th century, he considered it to be one of his less successful pieces. It's fair to say that history has proved him wrong...

'The Dance of the Sugar Plum Fairy' still sent shivers down Josephine's spine… and on this occasion, prompted a thump in her stomach too. 'Ouch,' she groaned. Turning to Ed and clutching her heavily distended belly, she whispered, 'Something's certainly stirred the little one.'

'Quite a cultured child we've got on our hands,' he replied, laughing.

But the kicking continued. With every note, the pounding grew harder. Josephine picked up a programme and began to fan herself gently. An hour ago, she'd felt bitterly cold. Now, rivulets of sweat were starting to pour down her neck. This wasn't just a problem of temperature control – something wasn't right. A wave of acute pain rose from within her groin, crashing hard against her stomach walls, draining away all colour from her skin in the process. Even before she had time to recover, Josephine could sense another peak of discomfort on the horizon.

Unfortunately, she wouldn't get to see *The Nutcracker* after all. Something far more dramatic was taking place inside her body. Josephine and Ed Miller were about to give birth to a sugar plum fairy of their very own.

Sienna Rose Miller took her first bite of the Big Apple on 28 December 1981, just two days before her older sister Savannah would celebrate her third birthday. Josephine chose to name her second daughter after her favourite Italian city. She was also convinced her newborn daughter had a sienna-coloured tinge to her skin.

Although Sienna would later describe her parents as 'hippies', both Josephine and Ed hailed from quite conventional backgrounds. An American banker brought up in Pennsylvania, Ed Miller would make a most financially viable catch for any woman. 'My father is very smart and wise,' says Sienna fondly, but Ed was a far cry from the straight-laced and grey-suited city type you might imagine. He had made a fortune, and with it had come the keys to a world of fame, where he would regularly rub shoulders with rock stars and artists. Having secured several business interests in the tax haven of Bermuda, Ed moved into a Manhattan apartment round the corner from Mick Jagger's own playboy pad. The fact that Ed happened to be extremely handsome was also a bonus. Sienna would later boast to friends that her wonderfully slim and sculpted ankles were a direct inheritance from her father.

Something of a head-turner herself, Jo Miller had become a familiar face on London's wild-child party circuit. Born in Hull, she went on to live in South America, Monaco and London. 'She's led an extraordinary life,' admits Sienna. Of mixed South African and English descent, Jo's exotic good looks had landed the untiring socialite several modelling contracts. The pinnacle in her career was a cover for glossy high-society US magazine *Tatler*. 'My mum is beautiful,' coos Sienna of the woman she cites as one of her greatest influences. During Jo's 1970s heyday, plenty of young and eligible gentlemen would have agreed without hesitation.

Later in her career, Jo would work as a personal assistant for high-profile clients such as David Bowie. It was even alleged that the two were involved in a short-lived fling. British tabloids, however, would later put the dampers on the rumour, cruelly claiming it had been conjured up to give Sienna's family history some much-needed credibility. 'Bowie's London-based PR firm say their client cannot recall any relationship with "Josephine" – either personal or professional,' reported the *Daily Mail*. 'Bowie, of course, has led a colourful life and it is possible he may have forgotten about her.' The paper went on to interview Bowie's former wife Angie, who also claimed to have no recollection of a Jo Miller: 'We had an office in New York at the time, but David didn't have a secretary. There were a couple of girls who did things around the office from time to time, but neither of them fits the description of Sienna's mother and her name rings absolutely no bells with me at all,' she stated firmly. But whether the rumours were true or not, Jo Miller was certainly a feature of the celebrity world at the time.

Initially based on different sides of the Atlantic, Jo and Ed were phone acquaintances before they actually met. Both were engaged in business together, but soon discovered a mutual love of arts, film and theatre. Very quickly their conversations would drift away from work matters and into a world of literature, life dreams… and, later, love. 'Then one day he walked into her office and it was love at first sight!' smiles Sienna, herself a hopeless romantic.

It was decided the couple would marry and settle in New York. Most of Ed's business interests were firmly rooted in the States, and Jo didn't need much persuasion to start a new life in the rock'n'roll capital. After Sienna's birth, Jo spent a period of time at home looking after her new family. But it wasn't long before she had the urge to find a new creative challenge. 'My mum always worked when I was growing up,' recalls Sienna proudly.

When Sienna was just six months, Jo decided to enrol in drama school. 'She went there for six months after she had us,' explains Sienna. '[It was] out of curiosity... she is quite adventurous in that way. But neither of [my parents] was really involved in that industry.'

It wasn't long before Ed's work prompted a family move back to London. After moving between several locations, the Millers eventually set up home in the trendy West London district of Parsons Green. 'It's kind of single mothersville,' says Sienna of the area. 'Everyone has dogs and kids. It's sweet, like a village.'

Both Jo and Ed were determined their children should be brought up in a relaxed household — free from the shackles that earlier generations of parents had enforced on their offspring. Sienna's parents had been children of the Swinging Sixties, brought up with the bohemian lifestyle and schools of thought that flourished in that decade. Sienna's childhood made a lasting impression on her. 'I was brought up in a very creative environment,' she says today, with a smile. 'Mum took us to the ballet, the opera, the theatre, and we always had music on full blast. I have great memories of dancing around the house to *Madame Butterfly*. Everything creative was allowed and embraced by our parents.'

During the 1960s, Jo had been an early pioneer of exercise classes. She continued to teach in London and would frequently invite both Sienna and Savannah to join in. 'She does a mixture of yoga and the Alexander technique, which is very good for actors,' explains Sienna. 'I used to sit in on the classes when I was younger.' Given the tumultuous course of Sienna's personal life, these were skills that would later prove invaluable. 'It's a place you can go to and get a peace of mind. Having done it since a young age, it was like riding a bicycle. As soon as I do it for ten minutes, I can go back to a state of tranquillity, which is important because acting is quite a chaotic lifestyle. The Alexander technique was good for posture too. I found [that out] while I was studying walking, because it is a strength that I didn't have enough of at the time.'

Spurred by her love of theatre, Jo started working for the London branch of the Lee Strasberg Theatre Institute. It was famously dedicated to the values and ideals of method acting, and past alumni of the LA and New York schools have included Robert De Niro, Al Pacino and Marilyn Monroe. The latter even left 75 per cent of her estate to Lee Strasberg, citing the American theatre coach and director as an instrumental figure in both her professional and personal life.

Thanks to Jo's new job, the Miller household became a hub of an artistic scene. 'We always had artists, actors and musicians hanging around the house – wonderful creative people,' recalls Sienna. It hardly came as a surprise then, when aged just three a precocious Sienna announced to her parents that she wanted to be an actress. 'Apparently, I watched *Some Like It Hot* and said, "That's it. That's what I want to do,"' she giggles. 'I was quite outspoken as a child and I think I wanted to be a ballerina and everything, but acting was the thing that seemed to stick.'

Sienna didn't waste any time. No sooner had she declared her desire to tread the boards than she landed her first role – as the Angel Gabriel in the school nativity play.

Looking back, Sienna admits that she had been no different to any other child. 'I think [it's something] everybody does when you're young and you go and see plays and ballet. You want to be in a world that's like that, everyone does. And, because my mum was supportive of it, I never really relinquished that.' With hindsight, though, Sienna can clearly identify the path leading towards her acting career and says that it was inevitable she should end up working within that field, given the creative household that surrounded her. 'I think, if you're brought up in an environment like that, something like acting is easy to do.' She hesitates before adding, 'There is no way you can ever work in an office!

My sister is a designer now and we were very much drawn into artistic things. I went to the theatre and used to see these people dressing up and playing for a living and thought, That looks like a pretty good job. I know it's a cliché, but I can't remember honestly wanting to do anything else.'

As an inquisitive child, Sienna was fascinated by the variety of odd characters who would pass through her parents' front door. She would watch and mimic certain mannerisms, wondering exactly why people chose to conduct themselves in a certain way. She didn't know it at the time, but Sienna was already honing her craft. Even today, the diligent actress goes to great pains to research her characters thoroughly. Desperate to make her performance believable, she even adopts their physical appearance.

'I'm not shy,' she acknowledges. 'I'm definitely outgoing. I'm interested in people and how they behave, so I have always been fascinated by the idea of exploring all sorts of characters. Getting paid for doing it is a bonus. When I was younger, I would read a book and then be that character. It's wonderful to play all these different kinds of people and discover where they are coming from.'

It seemed life in the Miller household was nothing short of perfect. Ed's successful career ensured the family was financially stable, and Jo was shaping up to be the glamorous mum all young girls dream of having. Young

Sienna Miller had it all. But then one day Ed came home with news that would shatter his family's idyll forever. He was leaving Jo for another woman.

TWO

The Early Years

AFTER Jo discovered her husband had been having an affair, the couple agreed to separate. To make matters worse, the woman Ed had been fooling around with was one of Jo's closest friends. Potentially, this was an explosive situation. But, although Ed would later speak of an 'incredible amount of frustration' and 'ill-will' that had to be buried, Sienna recalls the whole scenario quite differently. Although aged only five at the time, she weathered her parents' marital storm quite comfortably. 'I'm sure I'm psychologically blocking stuff to do with my parents' split,' she reflects. 'All those feelings of abandonment and banished trust... But all I can remember is being excited about getting two Christmas stockings and living in two homes, and after an acrimonious divorce they're now good friends and go on holiday together.'

Within almost 12 months of the split, Ed Miller struck up a new relationship with the famous interior designer Kelly Hoppen and the pair later married. Kelly already had a daughter, Natasha, from a previous marriage. Now Sienna had a new stepsister. Born in Cape Town, crimson-haired Kelly was another South African who had defected to the UK. She says simply of her relationship with Ed, 'We met, we hit it off and it was an instant family.'

But, in light of Ed's commitments from his previous marriage, the relationship wasn't without problems. 'When you are in the throes of passion, you don't think about the complications. It was hard, though. Just think about it – Ed moved in with me and his tiny new stepdaughter, and his two daughters weren't too happy about that. Then they'd come home from school and Tash would feel weird. So it took a couple of years to find the balance, but, my God, we worked at it.'

Over time, Sienna grew to accept her new stepmum. She would visit her father's new family during the school holidays. On occasion, this would include stints at Elton John's place in the South of France. 'We've been together for so many years now,' says Kelly of her relationship with the Miller sisters. 'The girls grew up together, and I want to see them all do their own thing, I gave Sienna good advice. She wanted to go travelling and I said, "Why? You are the one kid who actually knows what you want to do."

So she studied acting and she's fine now. Savannah has just graduated from Central St Martins and she's doing stuff for Matthew Williamson so she's OK. Now it's little Tash's turn.' Sienna's younger sister is about to embark on a singing career. 'It's really strong stuff. Sienna came to hear her sing and cried for about five hours afterwards,' claims Kelly proudly.

Even though Ed and Kelly divorced in 2002, the four women often go out on shopping trips together and share style tips. 'We are all brutally honest with each other in the changing rooms and have a real giggle,' says Kelly, with a smile. 'They are always raiding my wardrobe, though, and whenever I have a clearout they have a field day. Sienna still has a pair of my Prada shoes and I know they are too small for her.' For her part, Sienna still counts her stepmum as a loyal friend: 'My ex-stepmother is an interior designer, so I can get stuff at cost,' she jokes. 'It's the upside of having a father who remarries a few times.'

Bizarrely, Kelly would later reveal that her marriage to Ed had ended after he joined a religious cult in the States. In a desperate bid to rescue her marriage, Kelly even went to watch an initiation ceremony at the cult. Unfortunately, her efforts were unrewarded when the cult leader hit her. 'They were in sheets and beads,' Kelly told *Tatler* magazine. 'We had to stand in a queue holding a flower. I was petrified. I was trying to patch up my marriage and find out what was happening to Ed. I even considered joining. When he reached me, the leader said,

"I've been waiting so long to meet you." I gave him the flower and he hugged me very hard. He hit me first with a peacock feather and then with his hand. The blow was so strong that I fell backwards and hit my head on a banister. Everyone thought it was fabulous.' Ed eventually moved to the Virgin Islands to marry a fellow cult member. 'Ed is much happier now,' says Kelly of an ex-husband she still considers to be a friend.

Overall, Sienna had been lucky. Having survived her parents' divorce relatively unscathed, she now belonged to two close-knit families. At home, Jo continued to do a stellar job in rearing her two increasingly beautiful daughters. 'My mum is a real Jewish mother even though she isn't Jewish!' says Sienna, with feigned goofiness. 'She cooks and clucks and takes care of me.'

Keen to give their daughter the best education possible, Jo and Ed had decided Sienna should be sent to boarding school. After a stint at a school in Salisbury, Wiltshire, she went on to attend Heathfield in Ascot, Berkshire – 'this quintessentially posh English boarding school', she recalls. With school fees set at £20,000 a year, this was education for a high-society elite. During her time at Heathfield, Sienna would compete in a skiing contest with British number-one alpine skier Chemmy Alcott and also struck up a friendship with Calum Best – just one indication of the swanky circles in which she was mixing. Quick to dismiss the idea that she was born with a silver spoon in her mouth,

Sienna proudly boasts that she was accepted to Heathfield on a bursary. 'So I wasn't as posh as everyone else!'

Initially, Sienna found it difficult to settle in. She'd grown accustomed to her carefree life at home and the introduction of rules and regulations came as a sobering shock. Her fellow pupils labelled her 'Squit', in reference to her petite frame. And, just as Sienna had enjoyed meeting the carousel of characters who frequented her parents' house, she quickly warmed to her new social circle. Her chameleon-like ability to adapt to different groups ensured she was never without friends. A member of the lacrosse team and the choir, she also developed her taste for acting by playing lead roles in the school productions of *Annie* and *Oliver!*. Sienna also credits boarding school with teaching her good manners and respect for fellow pupils. 'Boarding school teaches you freedom. You learn to share what you have and you bring each other up.'

As a teenager, Sienna was 'gawky' and a 'beanpole with braces', in her own words – a far cry from the elegant and waspish beauty who graces magazine covers today. 'God, I'm not being humble but at school, you know, braces, no breasts – which hasn't changed that much! Ha! I was really spotty and greasy as a teenager.'

What's more, she refers to her early fashion sense as appalling. 'When I was fourteen I had horrible style. Everyone's such a conformist at that age. You think you're not, but you always are. I went through this tomboyish stage where I wore lumberjack shirts and green jeans and then pink shirts and ripped jeans and we always all looked the same. As you get older, you try to be individual and fail miserably. I had pink and white streaks in my hair at one stage. And braces. A hideous contradiction.'

However, reports from her fellow classmates paint a completely different picture. Remarking on her inimitable sense of faultless style one girl complains, 'She somehow made you feel like you wanted to rush into your dormitory and change. But, even if you did, it just never quite worked like it did on her.'

Modest to the point of embarrassment, Sienna would often put herself down in front of others, and her habit for self-deprecation is something that continues to this day. Partly, it's a clever ploy to make those around her feel more comfortable. But there's also a sense that – incredibly – Sienna still doesn't realise quite how gifted she actually is.

Loud and extrovert, Sienna very soon found herself to be the centre of attention. As she grew more familiar with her surroundings, the cheeky teenager developed a daredevil streak for breaking all the rules. 'We used to do stupid, fun, girly things,' shrugs Sienna nonchalantly. 'Like pull tights over our faces and streak through the lacrosse pitch.' She also vividly recalls her first taste of underage drinking. 'I remember hitching up my horrid, long tweed skirt and sneaking off to Ascot to buy bottles of vodka. We'd drink it and then throw up. Then I snogged the gardener. He was quite good-looking and it was a daring thing to do in a school with two hundred girls – but it was pretty mild stuff.'

Perhaps Sienna's most embarrassing tale from her boarding school days was an incident involving a hormonal dog and an unsuspecting Domino's Pizza man. Waking up one morning with a thumping headache, Sienna decided to skip classes for the day and stay in bed. But it wasn't long before her appetite returned. Rather than venture into the dangerous world outside, she picked up the phone and ordered a takeaway pizza. Lounging around her room in nothing but an oversized T-shirt, Sienna flicked through various TV channels while she waited for her food to arrive. The only company she'd kept all day was with her pet spaniel.

The doorbell rang.

'I'm just coming!' shouted Sienna, as she stumbled to find her purse, buried beneath a mound of dirty laundry and essay notes. Hurried along by a saliva-inducing waft of melted mozzarella and freshly baked dough, she opened the door. But, as she went to pay the delivery man, something inexplicable happened. As if overcome by the smell of freshly cooked pizza, the dog started to hump her leg.

'I turn around, and before I know it he's pulled my shirt up around my head. And I've got no knickers on!' she exclaims, still cringing at the memory. 'So I'm standing there with my bare bum in the pizza guy's face! I just threw the money at him and shut the door. After that, whenever Domino's came around, they'd walk by my room and snigger.'

While Sienna's behaviour branded her as something of a rebel in the classroom, at home it would take a lot more to shock her open-minded parents. She recalls a time when she arrived home for the holidays with bright-orange hair. Her mum was in hysterics.

'What on earth were you thinking of, darling?' she managed to mumble, through her giggles.

Ed, however, greeted his daughter with a very different response. Concerned that her rebellion was a cry for help and a slight on his own inadequacies as a father, he sat her down for a heart-to-heart. 'What are you trying to change?' he begged Sienna with genuine concern. 'What are you unhappy about?'

Now it was Sienna's turn to control her laughter. 'My dad is American,' she later explained. 'And very analytical.'

But, while other teenagers were battling for their independence, Sienna was given hers on a plate. One time, aged 14, she came home and defiantly announced she would be meeting friends at the pub that evening. 'Fine, I'll pick you up at ten-thirty,' replied Jo calmly.

'There were never any boundaries at home,' says Sienna. 'Everything was fine as long as it was open and talked about, so there was never anything to rebel against.'

Sienna left Heathfield with three A-levels, although she scoffs at the idea she was a swot. 'I was in the middle. I was all right,' she smiles. At the time she was still only 17, a year younger than most UK college graduates. The young woman was unsure of what to do next, though. She considered drama school, but the thought of more institutionalised learning put her off. 'I just couldn't commit to being in one place for three years,' she sighs. 'At that time I was so relieved to be out of school, which I loved, but you know it's your first taste of freedom and the outside world and I didn't want to say that I would be in London studying for three years.'

A year earlier, during a trip to New York, Sienna was spotted by Tandy Anderson, owner of Select Models. She landed work for Abercrombie & Fitch, Coca-Cola and Prada. 'I did it because I couldn't commit to getting up at nine to work in an office,' she explains. But posing in front of a camera was never really a viable career option. 'It was a fun job, but I never loved it,' she says. 'I always find it a little bit mindless.' Besides, by her own admission, Sienna was never really cut out for the job. At five foot six, she fell woefully below the industry standard. 'I was far too short and not good at it!' she says with more than a modicum of modesty. 'It was never my sole career… It's the perfect part-time job,' she adds, however, 'and a great stepping stone into acting.'

Aware her daughter was desperately seeking some guidance, Jo intervened and suggested Sienna try for the Lee Strasberg Theatre Institute in New York. It was less conventional than other drama schools, and the idea immediately appealed to the young woman. 'I'd studied Brecht, Craig and Stanislavski at school and was very drawn to Stanislavski of the three. Plus I was eighteen and wanted a good excuse for moving to New York!'

Sienna enrolled for a six-month course – the perfect compromise for a girl too spontaneous to commit for anything longer. Immersing herself in the values and ideals of method acting, she describes her period of study as 'more therapy than training'. 'We did a lot of work trying to smell a lemon and feel the sunshine,' she recalls. 'I really enjoyed it and living in New York was fantastic.'

Sienna learned a lot during this intensive period and still employs the skills of method acting she picked up during her studies in much of her work today. She vividly recalls the moment she finally unearthed the roots of real characterisation. For several days, Sienna had been working on an emotionally distressing scene. Taking advice from her director, she began to assume every thought, feeling, mannerism and misery of her character. Suddenly, all the theoretic concepts she'd been studying fell into place, but she felt terrible. 'I just started feeling hideous and not knowing why,' she recalls.

'God, I feel really awful,' she said, taking the director aside. 'Maybe it's not working or something. What should I do?'

'Listen,' he said. 'You've been doing something really horrible. What do you expect?'

For a moment, Sienna stood silently mulling over his words. Slowly, it dawned on her that this was the effect she'd been working hard for months to create. 'When you've got a character who's not superficially fucked up but deeply fucked up, you've got to do that justice because there are people who can relate to that watching this. It was the first time I'd been really affected like that. It was a new feeling which I hope will come back one day...'

Once Sienna had finished her studies at Lee Strasberg, gaining an honours in Lamda Acting, she took off travelling around Central America for six months with her best friend of the time, Sapphire Dawney, who was also training to be an actress. Sienna eagerly grasped the opportunity to relax and learn about the world. 'I got kind of quite trampy and armpit-haired with dreadlocks,' she laughs. 'We went a bit potty. But that's what it's all about!'

By this point, Sienna had already appeared in stage productions such as *Independence*, *The Striker* and Anthony Minghella's *Cigarettes and Chocolate*. In 2000, she returned to London, fired up to give her acting career a shot. 'I thought that because I was young enough I could do a year of having an agent and see how it went and then if I wanted to go back to drama school I always could.' As it turned out, after making her decision, Sienna would never look back. 'I was very lucky actually and I'm quite glad. I think it worked that I didn't go [to drama school]. I think you are quite unconscious of any competition if you haven't been round drama schools and all of that. It's a great experience actually doing it.'

Years earlier, Sienna had boldly invited an acquaintance – Dallas Smith, her agent to this day – to see her perform in a school production of Sheridan's *School For Scandal*. Newly confident from her travels, she decided to reintroduce herself to Dallas. 'I was so obnoxious. I told him that, if he put me up for five things and I didn't get any of them, he need never talk to me again.'

Sienna eagerly took to her new social life in London. She quickly became a familiar face on the party circuit and enjoyed a fling with Charlie Gardner (a former flame of It Girl Tamara Beckwith) and the then relatively unknown actor Orlando Bloom. What's more, according to tabloid reports, Princess Anne's son Peter Phillips had begged for Sienna's phone number after spending an evening with her. Sienna remains coy about her social exploits. 'A friend of mine was organising parties. We were young, just having fun.' Around this time, Sienna also struck up a relationship with smooth operator Calum Best. The pair first met when Sienna was 16. She was apparently smitten with the socialite and the pair became pen pals when he eventually moved back to LA. Several years later, Calum moved back to London and was in search of a place to live. Sienna offered him her spare room and the pair became flatmates. By this point, however, their relationship was purely platonic.

Fortunately, her riotous period didn't last long and Sienna soon settled into a two-year relationship with her first boyfriend, David Neville. A former investment banker and model, he now co-owns the cult jeans company Rag & Bone. 'I met him when I was seventeen at a party and we were friends for a couple of years, then we got together,' she told reporters at the time. 'I'm very happy.'

Sienna was smitten and still counts him as the 'other' love of her life.

After returning from a Valentine's Day weekend in Rome, Sienna was due to audition for a role in a new offbeat American TV police drama, *Keen Eddie*. It was tipped to be the biggest TV craze since *Friends*, and this was no bit part for the young actress. Her head still floating in the clouds, Sienna breezed into the audition without a care in the world. 'I was completely in love and I just walked into the audition with a "whatever" attitude,' she recalls. Executive producer Simon West (also responsible for *Lara Croft: Tomb Raider*) was taken aback by her nonchalance. 'Later he said he called me back because I gave the impression that I didn't care whether or not I got the part,' Sienna reveals. The whole audition process was, apparently, quite straightforward. 'My agent put me up for the audition and they wanted someone young and Notting-Hilly – basically quite like me – so I was just very lucky, actually.' Only later would the sheer scale of the project dawn on her. 'The people involved are really good,' she told friends. 'It's quite daunting, actually.'

Sienna was cast as token eye-candy Fiona, opposite Mark Valley's Eddie Arlette. Filmed in London, the series followed the progress of a New York detective who had been banished from the capital after a drugs bust went wrong. Sienna explains her role: 'Fiona is twenty, from Notting Hill and quite arty and opinionated. She's irritated by Eddie who's very "New York". He moves into my flat, after my mother rents the place out to him, thinking I'm away at university. He shows up, and he threatens to tell on me if I don't let him stay. Of course, he has a dog and I have a cat. They fight; we fight.'

The *New York Daily News* called Sienna a 'knockout blonde'. However, reviews for the series were mixed and, despite great expectations, it was soon axed. Sienna remained characteristically upbeat about the whole episode: 'It opened up the American market and that is very hard to penetrate. As a result of doing that I got an American agent. It was great to have something in America,' she says with a shrug, before adding, 'but also great not to have to live out the seven-year option they had on us.'

Back in the UK, Sienna signed up with PFD – a talent agency based in London's theatre district, Drury Lane. Shortly afterwards, she scored a major role as Stacy in a six-episode comedy series called *Bedtime*, written and directed by Andy Hamilton (responsible for *Drop the Dead Donkey*) and produced by Hatrick for the BBC. The drama was set in the bedrooms of three houses on an average London suburban street. Each night, viewers would be party to the different night-time rituals undertaken by the respective households during the last half-hour of their day.

The show boasted a stellar cast. 'You know, to be cast in something with Alun Armstrong, Sheila Hancock, Timothy West and Adam Paul Harvey was great,' enthused Sienna at the time. 'It's just a fantastic script – very witty

26

and clever. We'd be in the studio all day, with a fake moon coming through, and then we'd go out for lunch and there'd be glaring sunlight – it was quite disorientating, but so much fun.'

Getting into character proved a doddle for Sienna. Her character Stacy was a 17-year-old model trying to break into TV and film – not too far removed from Sienna's own situation, then! 'Stacey's seventeen and very confident and ambitious, but as the series goes on you see more of her vulnerable side. I loved playing a character who is different. I think a lot of "young girl" parts are very similar – a young girl in love – and it's rare to find a character who's got her own thing going on.' The show aired in August and September 2002 on BBC1.

Meanwhile, offers of modelling work continued to trickle in. Although Sienna wasn't actively seeking jobs, she wasn't about to knock back an opportunity to earn some extra cash. In 2002, she was invited to appear as Miss September in the famous Pirelli calendar. She was photographed naked on the back of a donkey and admits the shoot was 'quite raunchy'. But she hastens to add there was nothing gratuitous about the nudity. 'Bruce Weber was the photographer. I knew he'd make it look artistic. Even her parents approved. 'Dad loved it, believe it or not,' she quips.

However, not all of Sienna's past modelling assignments are likely to make her portfolio. In March 2003, for example, she posed semi-naked for lads' mag *Maxim*. ('I have fielded quite a few requests for those photos, but Sienna's people don't want to see them published again, so I don't think you'll get permission to use them,' said the agent for the LA-based photographer responsible for the shots) A year later, men's style magazine *GQ* attempted to use similarly revealing shots in a feature. Sienna's PR company threatened the magazine would forfeit any future access to their client roster if publication went ahead. According to freelance photographer John Stoddard, he received several tearful phone calls from Sienna and even more aggressive ones from her publicist. Eventually, he relented – and lost £25,000 in the process.

For a brief period, Sienna considered returning to college. 'A part of me misses writing essays,' she complained. But she soon changed her mind: 'Realistically, I don't think [going back to school] is going to happen because I'm loving what I'm doing so much. But I'm so young. I forget how young I am.' By now, she was determined to pursue a career in acting. In 2003, she attended several Oscar parties with her boyfriend David Neville. It was her first experience of Hollywood glamour and the fledgling actress was visibly overwhelmed. 'We were standing about trying to be cool but really we were like, "Aaah!", she laughs. 'I felt like, "God, what the fuck am I doing here?" I was hiding in the bushes, smoking and watching and giggling.'

Two years later, Sienna would find herself among the elite, considered a star in her own right. She was about to become an overnight celebrity. Unfortunately – and much to her chagrin – her success owed very little to her acting achievements. Sienna Miller would find fame by virtue of the man she happened to fall in love with: a Hollywood actor by the name of Jude Law.

THREE

Debut on the Silver Screen

WHEN Sienna first arrived back in London, she mentally mapped out an acting career that would focus mainly on the stage. Film and TV work barely factored into the equation. But after endless waitressing and temping jobs, she quickly realised that any acting work was better than none. 'When I first decided to be an actress, all I ever wanted to do was theatre,' she admits. 'Then you get offered TV or film and you just need to do it. I kind of got caught up on a wagon that I never intended to get on.'

One afternoon, out shopping with friends, Sienna received an excited phone call from her agent. 'You're not going to believe this, Sienna!' he exclaimed excitedly, 'but you've been asked to test for the new Matthew Vaughn movie.' Sienna had been a big fan of *Lock, Stock and Two Smoking Barrels* and Matthew Vaughn was one of her favourite directors. 'What's more,' continued her agent, 'Daniel Craig and Michael Gambon have both been cast in the film.'

Sienna gasped. Had she been asked to conjure up a dream list of actors she'd love to work with, both those men would feature in her Top 10.

Based on a book by John L Connolly about British gangsters, *Layer Cake* was a largely male-dominated movie. Sienna's character Tammy, a flirty East End seductress, would provide some visual light relief. When Sienna arrived at her screen test, she was nervous. She'd never appeared in a film before, let alone alongside some of the biggest names in UK cinema. Casting director Jina Jay quickly recognised the young star's potential, though. 'I think Sienna is tremendously talented,' she said later. 'She's got something I find very interesting on screen, something intangible, and I think, if she marries that with good material and fantastic directors, she'll do her training that way.'

As it turned out, Sienna's part was only small, requiring her for just five days on set. 'It was a real boys' set!' she says of the filming. 'There was a lot of yelling and laughing at each other. I felt like the honorary girl.' Most of her time was spent frolicking in Agent Provocateur underwear and gyrating her hips in front of a camera lens. Sienna refers to Tammy as 'a complete slut... Part of me was nervous about playing someone who was that obviously sexual and tarty, but once we got on set all of those worries disappeared because it was such a laugh.'

Sienna was under no illusions about her role, and was fully aware that it served very little dramatic purpose whatsoever, summing it up as 'very gratuitous and slightly pointless… It was what it was. She is what she is. She's the girl.' But there was no way the ambitious actress was about to turn down an opportunity to work with 'all those wonderful British actors'. Besides, what woman would pass up the chance to be flung on a bed by Daniel Craig?

'Aghhh! You can only imagine what it was like! I loved being flung on to the bed. It wasn't difficult – I could think of worse people to be flung on beds by,' she winks mischievously. 'He's really rugged. He's beautiful but not a novice. He's a real man, isn't he? Great eyes. Ol' blue eyes.' Innocent at the time, these were comments Sienna would later regret when the tabloids linked her romantically with Craig.

Even though *Layer Cake* had hardly been a screen debut to write home about, it put Sienna in good stead for her next big-screen appearance in *Alfie*, a Hollywood remake of the classic 1960s movie that had helped to make Michael Caine a star. 'My first Hollywood film could so easily have been *Scream 4*,' jokes Sienna, looking back now. 'I was reading for films like that, so I feel very lucky that I ended up with a great part in *Alfie* and not playing a teenager.'

Transplanted to the streets of Manhattan, the update would star Jude Law in the lead role of lothario Alfie, alongside Jane Krakowski (the secretary Elaine in *Ally McBeal*), Oscar winner Maria Tomei and Susan Sarandon as his various love interests. Sienna auditioned for the role of Nikki, the 'young nightmare' desperate to win Alfie's inconstant heart. Although she could barely recall the original film, Sienna was instantly attracted to the script.

'The thing that stood out for me most was the comedy and how incredibly English it was,' she enthuses. 'It was a story I could really relate to, because *Alfie* is so London. I was quite impressed that two Americans had written it and managed to pull it off. It's got elements of absolutely every emotion in it, which is great. And the journey Alfie goes on is really interesting. It's kind of like he's living this untouchable, very confident, perfect life, [living] every man's dream.'

Sienna was desperate to land the role and claims she pestered director Charles Shyer on a daily basis, begging him to let her have a chance. 'I can do it,' she insisted. 'I promise.'

Initially, the studio had been keen to cast a big name, but soon relented. However, Charles Shyer recalls the scenario quite differently. He even thought she was American, her accent was so good. 'She read three sentences and I knew she was the one,' he says of Sienna's audition. 'I filmed a screen test with her and Jude and, when he and I watched it, we were just blown away; not just by her breathtaking beauty on screen but also by her real, rare acting ability. Playing Nikki is a hard part, it really is. Sienna is beautiful and she can act. There are a lot of girls who we all know who are beautiful but can't act – she can act.'

When Charles eventually called to offer Sienna the part, she could barely contain her excitement. Eager to start work on the project immediately, she rushed out and hired a copy of the original film. She confessed to Charles that, although she'd seen the movie before, she could barely recall the details and hadn't really understood what was going on. 'I think I was too young,' she told him, with refreshing honesty.

But, when she eventually sat down to watch the film, she had to switch off halfway through. 'I was quite shocked by the cruelty of [Alfie's] character,' she shudders. 'I mean there is absolutely no way that men would get away with talking to women the way that Michael Caine's character does in the original. In the new version, Jude's character still sleeps around, but he shows a more vulnerable side. The characters are more developed and Alfie's relationships with women are more intense. I think Jude's Alfie also has more charm – he's funny and cheeky.'

Comparing the two different scripts, Sienna noted, 'The main difference between the two films is the way that women have progressed since then. It's empowering for women to see how far we've come. It's an enormous leap from the Sixties to now. Women would just not allow men to speak to them like that or treat them in this way. [In our version] they end up empowered and he is the one with the wake-up call at the end of the film.'

Sienna was particularly impressed by Susan Sarandon's character, Liz. 'Susan Sarandon has the dream part. She plays this strong, wonderful, sexy woman who stands up to Alfie. She's rich, in control and very in touch with her sexuality.' Herself a victim of typecasting, Sienna found it refreshing to see such an unusual choice of casting. 'I think it's great to see an older actress getting such a fantastic part. For once she's not playing the mother, she's not playing the grandmother and she's not playing the cancer victim. She's playing a gorgeous, sexy woman with a tattoo of Pablo Picasso on her breast.'

Sienna's own character Nikki may have been more frivolous, but she certainly wasn't any less complex. Finally, the ambitious actress had a creative challenge on her hands. 'She is totally fucked up,' said Sienna with some degree of glee. 'But for an actress to get to initially be the perfect girl and then lose it like she does was great.' After reading through the script at home, Sienna felt that several aspects of her character weren't quite right. Charles Shyer welcomed her enthusiastic comments and the pair sat down to rewrite the part together. 'On paper it wasn't quite right,' says Sienna. 'But we worked it out. She needed to be a complete psycho.'

Examining her character's motivation, she continues, 'I think for Nikki there is this guy who is very handsome and they have an instant attraction. That's the first thing. And then there is some outrageous flirting. He's her match in a male form. She doesn't mean to fall for him like she does and reveal everything she does. But then she genuinely believes it is going to work and that she doesn't need to take her medication because here is this guy that will save her. She really believes that they are the same kind of person but then she can't cope with it.'

Recognising Sienna's inimitable sixth sense for style, Charles invited her to help with some of the costumes. 'I was so blown away by her incredibly cool way of dressing that I got her to help style all the hip, young characters that make up the gang she's in when Alfie first meets her,' he told reporters.

Inspired by the 1960s roots of the film, Sienna drew on the fashions of that period for fashion ideas. She was keen to make Nikki a flamboyant dresser. 'We wanted to keep an element of the Sixties with my character and the styling of it,' she explains. 'It was a big collaboration between the make-up, the wardrobe, Charles and me. We all discussed what kind of things we wanted.' Unbeknown to Sienna, Charles had visualised her in the mould of 1960s starlet Julie Christie (star of *Far From the Madding Crowd* and *Don't Look Now*). He even asked the hair stylists to cut Sienna's fringe in a similar style. When asked about the comparison, Sienna laughs endearingly. 'He did mention Julie Christie, but I don't think he wanted to put me in a category that might limit me.' At the time, Charles kept his vision to himself, and instead encouraged Sienna to explore the character herself and make her own decisions.

Another aspect of the film that appealed to Sienna was

the musical score. Again, this was very much influenced by the 1960s, with music written by Dave Stewart and Mick Jagger. Describing herself as a 'rock'n'roll girl', a star-struck Sienna relished the opportunity to meet both artists. 'I love The Rolling Stones and I think Dave Stewart is fantastic,' she cooed. Invited down to the famous Abbey Road Studios, Sienna admits she pinched herself several times just to check she wasn't dreaming. The scene was incredible; in one corner sat the piano The Beatles used when they were recording *Sergeant Pepper*, while in another Mick Jagger was tinkering about with a harmonica. Dave Stewart, meanwhile, was sat quietly strumming his guitar. When Sienna eventually summoned up the courage to interrupt and introduce herself, she was relieved to discover Mick was not one for airs and graces. 'I was incredibly overexcited when I first met him,' she giggles with a schoolgirl innocence. 'But Mick Jagger is not the kind of person who'd allow you to be star struck, he is far too warm and down to earth.' Had she been given half a chance, Sienna would even have appeared in the film's accompanying music video. 'I was in Venice when they recorded the video but had I been there I would definitely have tried to muscle in.'

Although Sienna didn't base her character on anyone in particular ('I would normally bolt if I saw too much of Nikki in anyone!' she joked), she found it easy to imagine the type of person Nikki would be. Her experience of living in America helped greatly in this instance. 'People are more accepting about being fucked up over there. In England everybody represses everything and if they are fucked up they keep it to themselves.'

But Sienna was anxious not to make her character a cliché. Quite often, her desperate attempts to win over Alfie are sad and pitiful. Sienna wanted to illustrate that emotional vulnerability: 'The film was hard because the character is so complex. I wanted to do her justice and not be a cliché of nuttiness. I wanted to keep a certain degree of subtlety.'

Of all the scenes Sienna shot, her break-up with Alfie was the hardest to do. Shooting started on the Thursday and continued until Tuesday the following week, with a break for the weekend. 'This thing dragged on and on for some reason,' complains Sienna. 'We did a lot of coverage, because we wanted to get it from a lot of angles.'

By the time the crew finished filming on Friday, Sienna was exhausted. Although everyone was in desperate need of a rest, she would have preferred them to simply carry on. Waiting to resume filming the following week was even more torturous. 'I just remember feeling crap for that weekend,' she recalls.

Sitting quietly at home on the sofa, she couldn't help but mull over her fictitious break-up. It was almost as if she were enduring the heartache herself. 'It penetrates, it really does,' she shudders. 'You go over and over this hideous break-up and it definitely gets under your skin.' It was a difficult process and something Sienna struggled to deal with. 'It did get a bit manic,' she admits. But it was definitely a learning curve, albeit a rapid one. 'The environment on that set was very conducive to making it as real as possible. It did affect me. It was tough.'

On top of the emotional demands foisted on Sienna, her role was also physically challenging. Once again, a certain degree of nudity was required for the part. In one scene, Sienna cooks dinner in nothing but Ugg boots and a thong. Charles discussed the scenes carefully with Sienna and gave her the option of rewriting them, if she felt at all uncomfortable. But Sienna insisted: nudity formed an integral part of the role and being a professional she refused to tone down the script for fear of diluting its impact. 'That scene was so desperate,' she explains. 'She'll try anything to make him [Alfie] stay. I felt it would be such a desperate thing to do and it would make people uncomfortable, because you're like, "Oh, God, don't! Oh no." It definitely works in that scene.'

Sienna was already wary of being cast as 'the pretty face' and the token 'blonde babe'. Although her critics might claim otherwise, there was more to Sienna than pin-up potential. 'I don't have a problem with nudity as long as it's relevant and not gratuitous,' she claimed defiantly. 'I've made some mistakes in the past and I know *Layer Cake* doesn't stand up to that, but I've done both films and I'm proud of them.'

The subject had obviously struck a raw nerve, for she went on to blast certain journalists for questioning her integrity as a serious actress. 'I had one journalist who read me a list of these actresses who won't do nudity and their reasons why and then sat back waiting for me to say something. I was looking at her and it was like, "What? So I'm a crap horrible tart then?" As an actress I feel that if you start to impose your own inhibitions then you are not doing your job. I'm fascinated by people who are extrovert, so I guess I've got a lot more nudity to come. My breasts will feature again in a few films!'

Although it's hard to imagine, Sienna does feel nervous stripping off in front of the cameras. It's not something she does to grab attention and, despite having an almost flawless figure, she'd rather not flaunt it to the world if at all possible: 'There are times when you are self-conscious and you would probably not prance around in a G-string and a pair of boots, as I did in *Alfie*, in front of a crew of men!'

She also denies that her body looks as good in real life as it does on screen. 'It's all manufactured,' she says matter-of-factly. 'Although it is fun to play sexy, it does take four hours of airbrush body paint and all the rest of it. Seriously, they spray you all over with foundation so they get rid of every little lump and bump and then highlight you with a bit of shimmer to make your boobs look bigger and your bum look better. All the dimples go and the light is perfect. It's not really that way normally.'

Many would argue that Sienna had the perfect figure, but the lady herself would be quick to disagree. 'That's very flattering, but I don't feel conscious of it,' she says modestly.

'I'd like to be voluptuous. I would like bigger breasts. I've got cellulite on my bum and some stretch marks on my side.' Despite being a tiny size 8, Sienna confessed she was extremely unhealthy and never watched what she ate. 'I'm pretty unhealthy, actually. I've got to start eating more vegetables and fruit, but I'm a bit of a junk-food queen.' Sienna's old housemate, Hannah Sandler, confirms: 'If you'd seen our fridge, you wouldn't have believed it. In my section it was all healthy food, but in Sienna's it was mostly chocolate, butter and fattening stuff.' During photo shoots, Sienna would constantly munch on sweet treats such as M&Ms or jelly babies and, if she wasn't snacking, she'd be smoking. 'They're my vice! I love my ciggies.' Worse still, Sienna boasted that she never exercised. 'Oh, God! I should – I want to be healthy,' she insisted unconvincingly. 'I do yoga but I don't think I could ever do aerobics – far too energetic!'

Even the mere suggestion that Sienna might be considered a sex symbol makes her flinch. 'I find it very embarrassing because I'm so desperate to be taken seriously,' she admits. 'As a girl you get labelled and I suppose that's inevitable, but I try to fight that as much as I can.' In fact, her idea of sexiness bears very little resemblance to the male stereotype so frequently played out in films. 'Men's traditional view of sexiness isn't sexy,' she claims. 'It shouldn't be so obvious: push-up bras and mini skirts? Sexiness is when people are comfortable with themselves. I think being able to hold your own in an intellectual conversation. Feeling like you don't need a man to complete you. Just feeling independent. Just feeling good with yourself is empowering.'

No doubt about it, men found Sienna hugely attractive. But she quickly became the envy of pretty much every woman too, as she would be starring alongside British cinema's number-one heartthrob Jude Law. Born on 29 December 1972 in south-east London, Jude (whose real first name is David) dropped out of school to star in the TV soap opera *Families*. Following a successful stage career, he went on to make his name in the movies with films such as *Gattaca*, *The Talented Mr Ripley* and *Cold Mountain*.

Sienna had seen plenty of Jude's films, but the thought of starring opposite a Hollywood star in no way fazed her. 'The stage I'm at, I'm so desperate to work that I wouldn't start researching anyone,' she joked, before adding more seriously, 'I think you get a sense from meeting people as much as from the work they've done.' But, even if she wasn't prepared to show it in public, Sienna was secretly looking forward to her on-screen tryst with the gorgeous star. (Even her mother Jo was excited!) 'All I could think about was that I was going to have to kiss Jude Law,' she says on her reaction to landing the role.

Rumour had it that Sienna marched straight up to Jude and gave a lengthy and almost sycophantic speech about how honoured she was to work with him. 'She wanted him to be her mentor and said that she was sure she would learn from him during filming,' claimed one source. 'At first I think Jude thought she was just making fun of him, but she wasn't.'

Charles Shyer had his own version of events to report. 'There was an instant chemistry, but it was a little lopsided because she was a little gaga,' he told journalists. 'She had told me, "You don't understand; growing up, Jude Law was such a big deal, I had his picture on my pinboard." And so she was really highly nervous.'

Perhaps unsurprisingly, neither story was true. Fond of playing tricks on Sienna, Charles couldn't resist feeding gullible journalists a pack of lies. 'He's such a fucking liar!' Sienna screamed through fits of laughter, when she heard what Charles had said about her meeting with Jude. 'He does this in interviews to wind me up. I swear I did not have a poster of Jude on my wall.'

Nevertheless, the couple struck up a friendship and, before filming had wrapped, Jude and Sienna were an item. Sienna was reserved in her comments about those first moments of attraction. 'We rehearsed very intensely,' she smiled. For his part, Jude was bowled over by both her talent and beauty. 'It blew me away when I first saw her on camera. I just hadn't seen anything like it. She is extraordinary,' he gushed.

Early on, the new companions also took up dance classes, which Sienna describes as 'an incredible way to fall in love'. She would boast to friends about Jude's grasp of choreography. 'He's such a great dancer already,' she cooed. 'He hasn't stepped on my toes once.' Her mother quickly noticed a change in her daughter. While she'd always been of a sunny disposition, now it was almost impossible to wipe the permanent grin from her face. 'I'm having so much fun at the moment. Everything's so exciting, I feel overwhelmed, I don't feel twenty-one,' she enthused. Everyone around Jude and Sienna could see they were falling in love. 'There was an immediate electricity, on screen and off,' recalls Charles Shyer. 'I feel a little like Cupid – if I hadn't cast Sienna, they probably wouldn't be together.'

From a professional point of view, Sienna admired the way Jude handled the role of Alfie. 'Jude has a lot of that London, cool vibe, which is relevant to Alfie,' she noted. 'He also has the charm and the charisma that makes Alfie magnetic to women.' But Sienna had no difficulties in differentiating between fiction and real life. Her love affair in front of the cameras was nothing like the romance blossoming off screen. For starters, her taste in men was very different to Nikki's. 'I've met them [men like Alfie], but I've never stayed talking to them for very long. I've got a good radar. Some women have this sick thing where they're kind of drawn to men who don't treat them very well. It happens a lot when you're younger. I remember going out with some complete schmucks when I was a teenager, but you learn.'

Sienna describes her ideal man as 'a nice guy that makes me laugh'. 'I'm not particularly fussy,' she shrugs. 'But, if you can sit there and fall off your chair laughing with someone, I'll tell you what, it's the best thing in the world.' Given Jude's comedy performance in *Alfie*, Sienna had obviously found her match.

Although careful at first to keep their romance under

wraps, the couple eventually decided to come clean. Sienna had been booked in to do a photo shoot for the American society magazine *W.* Unannounced, Jude turned up midway through to join Sienna for lunch. He agreed to appear in several of the photographs, giving the magazine a priceless exclusive. 'It was supposed to just be a shoot for Sienna and then Jude suddenly stopped by and they had lunch together. We got some great shots out there,' said a representative.

Once Jude and Sienna announced their romance publicly, an extraordinary media furore ensued. The attention paid to the fledgling couple's personal life was so great it almost eclipsed their film performance. Despite torrential rain and bad weather, thousands of fans turned out to greet the couple at the *Alfie* premiere in Leicester Square. Only a few weeks previously, Sienna had turned out for her *Layer Cake* premiere. She was extremely excited and loved the whole tradition of waltzing along the red carpet. 'I have never had a premiere before,' she cooed at the time. 'I was thrilled to be part of it. But I only worked a week for the film. I only have a very small part.' On that particular occasion, Jude was unable to accompany his new girlfriend. Instead, he stayed at home to babysit his children. Now circumstances were very different.

Sienna gasped as she stepped out of the car and on to the red carpet. She'd picked out a black camisole and matching trousers for the occasion; a look that was sexy, but understated. A cacophony of screams erupted as the crowd surged forward. For a girl who claimed to have only ever received 'two fan letters in my life', this was a whole new league of fame. Gripping Jude's hand tightly, she stepped forward. 'You can do this,' he whispered. After an initial rush of apprehension, Sienna took a deep breath and composed herself. Within a matter of minutes, she was happily chatting to fans and signing autographs. When the time came to enter the auditorium, it was almost impossible to drag her away!

A whole cast of celebrities had gathered to see the film, including Sienna's new pal Mick Jagger, Dave Stewart, Bob Geldof and ex-All Saints singers Nicole and Natalie Appleton. Jude admitted to guests that he'd been nervous about taking on the role of Michael Caine's seminal character. 'We were very true, I hope, to Alfie's opinions, his philosophies but what we had to alter was the world around him. The women in that world have changed more than men in the last forty years. I'm very proud of it and I just hope other people enjoy seeing it as much as I did making it.' Although he wasn't able to make the premiere, Michael Caine had given the remake his seal of approval and described it as a 'form of flattery'. According to Charles Shyer, the knighted actor had even offered advice on the casting. 'We were at a dinner party together and he was the first person to say to me Jude Law was right for the part.'

In spite of this welcome vote of confidence, Jude confessed that playing a womanising character, with whom he felt he had nothing in common, was extremely exhausting. 'I play this guy with a smile, on an up and on a buzz, which is not me at all,' he laughed. 'I had to maintain it for seventeen hours a day, six days a week for four months.'

Sienna agreed that she much preferred the real Jude to his fictional character. 'The real Jude is nicer than Alfie, he's got all his good points, he's very charming, but he's not a misogynistic bastard.'

The following day, pictures of the couple were splashed across the tabloids. Sienna's rise to fame had been meteoric, to say the least. She remained sceptical about all her instant success, wary that it had all happened overnight. '*Alfie* was a big film shooting in London and, because there's such a thirst for all that media stuff in London, it was very strange… For everyone, including myself, it's been a bit weird that it wasn't a gradual progression. And it became even more because of Jude and everything.'

The public quickly accepted Sienna. She was young, beautiful and seemingly the perfect complement to Jude Law. Wherever they went in public, people would stop and offer the couple congratulations. During Wimbledon, Jude had offered to take Sienna to a Tim Henman match. Sienna was extremely excited about the opportunity not only to see one of her sporting heroes play, but also to spend some quality time with Jude. But if she'd expected a peaceful day out, then she was in for a shock! The couple positioned themselves discreetly in the stands, but it wasn't long before several eagle-eyed crowd members spotted them. Within minutes the entire crowd were serenading the romantic couple with lines from 'Hey Jude'. Sienna giggled. Normally she'd be embarrassed, but right now no one could topple her happiness.

Sienna was aware that from now on people would be making judgements not only on her acting ability, but also on her suitability as Jude Law's new squeeze. 'I do feel an enormous pressure because there is so much curiosity about me. I'm at the stage where I'm on the brink of being judged massively, and that's a terrifying thing,' she shuddered. 'But I've never had any doubt that this is what I want or should be doing… Until I get my first review, of course, and turn to breeding horses. Not that I know the first thing about breeding horses!'

Unlike most couples, Jude and Sienna had forfeited the luxury of enjoying their blossoming love in public. Himself a seasoned celebrity, adept at dealing with the press, Jude was more than happy to help Sienna acclimatise to her new environment. 'Jude had been through it and was supportive.' Initially Sienna enjoyed the thrill of escaping persistent photographers. 'It was kind of fun at first, ducking through alleyways, running out back doors and kitchens.' But the novelty soon wore off. 'It was exciting… for a week. I don't think anyone can realise the extent of what it is, until you're really in it.'

Seeking solace from the media circus, Sienna would often retreat to her mother's allotment. Jo had recently discovered a passion for the outdoors and, like her daughter, relished a taste of the simple life. 'She loves growing vegetables,' giggled Sienna. The two would often sit and natter about everything from haute-couture fashion to mundane household matters. 'I go down there with a bottle of wine and we just sit there, in the middle of London, and it's so peaceful. It's wonderful to have this green space that hasn't been built on and that they won't allow [anything] to be built on. It's a great little retreat where we can go and watch the plants grow.'

Only recently, Sienna had purchased her first home. Up until that point, she'd always lived with Jo but, sad as she was to leave, both knew it was time for Sienna to fly the nest. More than mother and daughter, Sienna and Jo were also best friends. 'I really, really miss home,' Sienna would later reveal. 'I lived with my mum for so long and it's hard. She looks after me so well and whenever I feel rubbish I go home. She's always trying to entice me back. We're best friends. She knows me so well. She can read my mind, so if you're feeling rubbish she'll bring you hot chocolate with marshmallows without even asking. She'll know just what comfort food you need.'

For months, Sienna's father Ed had been pressing his daughter to invest her earnings in either business or property. Knowing how flighty she could be with cash, he was concerned her income would be frittered away on frivolous activities. 'I'm not good with money,' she once confessed. 'My weakness is clothes and books. And one day I would love to buy [works by] Modigliani and Egon

Schiele.' She agreed with her parents that it was time to put down some roots and take a little responsibility for herself. 'The money I was earning from films and television was just disappearing on silly things like a vintage guitar that I haven't even played yet!' she told friends, shame-faced.

Sienna chose to buy her first flat in Notting Hill. After all, she was the archetypal west London girl! Chelsea, where her mother still lived, was also reassuringly close by. 'I've just finished decorating and it looks very oriental,' she revealed, with excitement. 'Lots of hot colours, Moroccan mirrors and antique painted doors and old Chinese trunks. Now I want to transform the patio. I've been growing lavender and I'm going to buy a lemon tree and cultivate lots of herbs.' She had the boyfriend, she had the burgeoning career and now this enviable young female had her own home.

Very soon, Sienna would find these safe havens an indispensable source of sanity. Although the capricious media doted on the love-struck couple at the time, it could swiftly change tack. Even a sniff of scandal could cause the papers to switch allegiance. Had the press only been concerned with Jude and Sienna's relationship, they would have quickly lost interest. But, unfortunately, Jude had a history that refused to disappear and blend into the background. There was a third party involved in this real-life drama – Jude's wife, Sadie Frost.

FOUR

Jude and Sadie

THE early 1990s was an exciting time for British cinema – not necessarily because of the calibre of films being made, but because a new jet set of effortlessly cool actors and actresses was emerging, and this new guard of British thespians was taking up more and more column inches in the press. Elsewhere, led by bands like Blur, Pulp and Oasis, the Britpop scene was exploding. Names such as Stella McCartney and Kate Moss tripped off the tongue of every high-brow fashionista worldwide. The style press were awash with stories of 'Cool Britannia' and not since the 1960s heyday of Carnaby Street and Mary Quant had London been such a hip place to live.

Quite unintentionally, Jude Law found himself at the

centre of this scene, though, given his public-school and straight-laced background, he was hardly a likely candidate. His father Peter was a primary-school teacher, while his mother taught English to refugee children. Both were heavily involved in amateur dramatics and now run their own theatre company in France. Jude initially attended a local comprehensive school in south-east London, but was disturbed by the levels of violence and bullying there. He later referred to it as 'a nightmare place, really aggressive and racist'. After suffering taunts for his 'posh' accent, at 14 he moved to Alleyn's public school in upper-class Dulwich.

But by the age of 12 he had already started mixing with a group of actors destined to become tomorrow's tabloid darlings. After enrolling at the National Youth Theatre, he befriended a young Jonny Lee Miller, who would later make his name as Sick Boy in *Trainspotting* and as Angelina Jolie's first husband. 'We used to meet in the holidays and do festivals and, because our initials are similar, we shared a room,' recalls Jude, with fondness. Years later, while auditioning for a role, Jude struck up a conversation with a rising actor called Ewan McGregor. Jude would later refer to both men as 'my dearest friends – there is never any competition, just understanding and respect'.

One of the biggest turning points in Jude Law's life would come in 1994 when he signed up to do the indie flick *Shopping*. A gritty urban drama, the film followed a group of thrill-seeking, disaffected youths, who passed their time stealing cars and ram-raiding shopping centres.

The film was universally panned, but it did allow Jude to forge important friendships with fellow cast members Sean Pertwee, Marianne Faithfull and – most importantly – Sadie Frost.

Five years Jude's senior, Sadie was a graduate of the Italia Conti Academy of Theatre Arts. Her most notable performance to date had been as Lucy Westenra in *Bram Stoker's Dracula* two years previously. In stark contrast to Jude, Sadie had enjoyed a very bohemian childhood. Sadie's mum was a ballet dancer-turned-barmaid who had been just 16 when she gave birth (Sadie even recalls her mum's 21st birthday party) and both her parents married three times. Her father was an artist who lived in a caravan. Sadie recalls travelling around Europe in a coach, dressed in nothing but a pair of pants. She was taken into foster care for a while until her mum was eventually given a council flat. '[It was] very wild, and full of change and moving around and different parents,' she recalls. 'I remember my childhood being fun. We played on the street a lot. It was exciting.' Arguably, however, such an unstable upbringing would have later repercussions on Sadie's own relationships. She admitted as much in later life: 'Yes, I wanted to have a family very early on. I like the security of having breakfast with someone. I like to know there's someone there when I'm going home in a taxi.'

When Sadie first met Jude she was married to Spandau Ballet's Gary Kemp (aged 16, Sadie had been a dancer in their video for 'Gold') and had a son, Finlay. Jude testifies that nothing happened between him and Sadie on set, but that romance blossomed once filming had ended. 'With Sadie and I, nothing happened until after the film, which is a good thing. We didn't want it to be a set affair.'

Initially, Sadie doubted her relationship with Jude would last. 'I didn't really think a man and a woman could live together properly – I'd only seen three-year relationships all my life.' But Jude was smitten. He even had the words 'Sexy Sadie' inked on his left forearm as a sign of his enduring love. The tattoo was a nod to the Beatles song as well as a reference to the purring star's femme-fatale sex appeal.

Jude and Sadie eventually married in 1997 (just weeks after Sadie was divorced from her previous husband) and had three children together; Rafferty, Iris and Rudy. The wedding took place on a barge on the Grand Union Canal, close by to the couple's notorious Primrose Hill stomping ground. Sadie wore a Galliano dress hastily borrowed from her good friend, super-waif fashion model Kate Moss. According to mutual friend Stella McCartney, the newlyweds were made for each other. 'It's real. You can see that it is. Sadie has a very motherly side as well as all the energy. So she's quite calm. Cuddly. She's a good mixture of everything. She finds the time to sit down and be a mother and a wife.' Jude and Sadie were officially the coolest couple. The fact they were talented, artistic and ethical made them even more appealing. 'They're both veggies!' exclaimed Stella in *Vogue* magazine. 'And we love that. Anti-fur, kind to animals – it's kind of cool that they're both young like me, and really passionate about it.'

Despite being just 22 when he first met Sadie, Jude quickly settled into family life. While other young stars his age were busy sowing their oats, Jude found pleasure in domestic pursuits. 'I never thought I had to forge a family, but it felt the most natural thing that ever happened to me – meeting someone and becoming a father,' he said at the time. Despite being married to one of the best-looking men in Britain, Sadie insisted that their marriage was very normal. 'He has that light that some people get round them,' she said. 'But I don't sit there going, "Cor! Look at him!" It's like looking through a magazine and seeing a really gorgeous photograph of Kate, in Fendi or something. I know what Kate looks like... She isn't that photograph! And it must be the same for Jude. He still looks in the mirror: he sees the stubble, he sees the pores, he sees the blackheads, he sees the veins that every single person on this planet has. He is good-looking just like millions of people are good-looking... but I think part of his attractiveness is that he doesn't really care, which is quite refreshing. And you're seeing the person in their dressing gown making a cup of tea just like any other family. And – you know – that person becomes very ugly when they haven't brought you tea, don't they?'

Desperate to spend time with his children, Jude vowed never to work abroad for long periods of time. While his career was important, family was his key concern. 'I'm happiest at home hanging out with the kids,' he told friends. 'Having a family has been my saving grace because

I don't work back to back on anything or I'd drive myself to an early grave with guilt and worry for my family, whom I'd never see.' At home, Jude and Sadie lived a very ordinary life. Initially, they refused to have a nanny, and called instead on the assistance of Sadie's younger sister. Jude would often spend evenings in reading bedtime stories to Raffy, and the couple would often rent a cottage in the countryside as a weekend retreat for the kids.

In 1999, Sadie and Jude went into business together, launching the production company Natural Nylon with friends Jonny Lee Miller, Ewan McGregor and Sean Pertwee. Their first film, the cult David Cronenberg-directed *eXistenZ*, starred Jude opposite Jennifer Jason Leigh. Jude admitted that being married to someone in the same industry could lead to an 'unstructured, unschedulable, rather chaotic lifestyle… And so it means double the trouble,' he explained. 'But equally there is support of it, an understanding of it. You are with someone who enjoys what you enjoy. You can talk about your work.' Jude admitted there were plus and minus points to such a relationship, but his remedy was simply to 'go with it, be practical and realistic'. Frost was equally upbeat about the obstacles facing their relationship. 'You know, you still have all the problems that relationships have. Sometimes it's exciting and wonderful, and then other times it's crazy and chaos and the children are screaming. But I couldn't really ask for anything more. Certainly I couldn't be more happy, really.'

But, while Jude and Sadie were keen to paint a picture of their lives as domestically mundane, the tabloids soon revealed quite a different story. Sadie had always possessed a wild streak and there was no denying she and Jude were top of every celebrity's party invite list. *Vogue* even referred to them as the 'crown prince and princess of the tight little London film/fashion/art crowd, the pair most wanted at everybody's party'.

In 1999, Sadie launched a fashion label with her pal Jemima French. Initially, the two women set out to sell items of fun scented lingerie. FrostFrench was a hit with consumers and what started out as a hobby soon became a business. Their fashion shows became the talk of the town. In one instance, Sadie replaced the conventional catwalk show with a play. 'It was about four girls who've all been sleeping with the same man – Rock Girl, Soul Girl, Book Girl, Cool Girl – and it was about how they dressed on their dates. Kate [Moss] was Cool Girl, and she started off dressing and undressing. Most stressful thing I've ever done,' she says. Sadie was welcomed into a fashion world with open arms and even more party invites began to appear on the doorstep.

The group of friends with whom Sadie socialised were tagged by the press as 'The Primrose Hill Set'. An icon for Cool Britannia, Sadie even appeared in the video for Pulp's anthemic single 'Common People'. While Jude would frequently accompany his wife to parties, reports were starting to filter through to the press that the serious and bookish intellectual was beginning to feel like a decidedly un-hip fish out of water. 'Sadie constantly criticised Jude and made fun of him,' a so-called insider sniped in a leak to the press. 'He spent years thinking that he's actually not really that cool, or that interesting, or able to compete with her friends. Jude is a solid, middle-class, quite boring bloke who likes architecture.'

At the time, Sadie was pregnant with the couple's third child, Rudy. She gave birth five weeks prematurely, with the baby weighing just 5lb 5oz, in September 2002. Sadie was out with Kate Moss when she suddenly went into labour. Jude was filming in America, but took the first flight home and arrived in time for the birth. He was granted only four days off set to spend with his wife and newborn child, putting even more pressure on an already fragile relationship.

Eyebrows had also been raised about Sadie's drinking habits. In 2000, she hit the headlines for being arrested by Berlin police after being trapped in a lift, allegedly drunk. Sadie made no attempt to deny her party-loving antics. 'I'm always the girl at the party who, within five minutes, has taken my heels off, hitched up my dress in my knickers, and probably spilled drink down my cleavage,' she told *Heat* magazine.

The wayward actress was placed in an even more compromising situation when her two-year-old daughter Iris was rushed to hospital for swallowing half an ecstasy tablet in October 2002. The incident took place at London's trendy members-only club Soho House, where family friends Pearl

Lowe and Supergrass drummer Danny Goffey were celebrating their son's sixth birthday.

Sadie realised something was wrong when she noticed Iris grimace after putting something in her mouth. She rushed over to see the toddler spit out half a grey tablet. Immediately, she tried to empty her daughter's mouth but it was already too late. Iris was rushed to hospital, where she was given a brain scan and had her stomach pumped. Officers from Scotland Yard confirmed the substance was ecstasy.

At the time, Jude was in Romania filming for *Cold Mountain* with Nicole Kidman. He was furious when Sadie called him to explain what had happened. The tabloid press seized on the opportunity to criticise Sadie for her hedonistic lifestyle, but she protested that she'd done nothing wrong: 'Jude and I aren't some rock'n'roll couple,' the actress and mother of four told the *London Evening Standard*. 'I still can't believe all this happened. I'm not a bad mum; nobody was taking drugs that afternoon. If I had seen anyone taking drugs that afternoon, I would have been out of the door immediately.' Instead, Sadie described the party as being full of 'mummies and grannies and cups of tea'. Even though Soho House was a nightclub, she'd seen no problem in taking her children there on a Saturday afternoon. 'Soho House didn't seem a particularly odd choice as a venue,' she explained, 'since at weekends they do all sorts of family-orientated events, child-friendly menus and a small cinema room. It wasn't a big party and, apart from the Supergrass element, it was celeb free.'

But reports, although unsubstantiated, suggested Jude blamed his wife for putting their children in a risky situation. He swore to boycott the venue and would persuade all his high-profile friends to do the same. At one point he even threatened to sue the club, but the couple eventually chose to drop any charges. 'What would it achieve?' Sadie concluded. 'I'm not going to start pointing fingers. Nick Jones, who owns Soho House, has called me and is very concerned. He has young children, too.' Nevertheless, Jude struggled to forgive his wife.

For her part, Sadie accused her husband for putting his career before his family. 'Acting is a very selfish job. The nature of it is you become self-obsessed, and I found that was detrimental to me as a person and as a mother,' she was once quoted as saying. This was a sore point, as Jude had always made an issue of doing quite the contrary. Cynics would argue that Sadie's floundering film career had more to do with it. While her own acting work had been thin on the ground, Jude had been inundated with offers.

Strains on the relationship grew worse when it was rumoured Jude and a newly single Nicole Kidman were having an affair. Photographs of the pair taken at a drunken American Independence Day party at the cast's Villa Zorile hotel had been circulated to the press. Scrutinising the shots, journalists noticed Jude had removed his wedding band. Both Nicole and Jude vehemently denied allegations of impropriety. Indeed, the leggy Australian successfully sued the *Sun* for libel. Jude even chose to stay away from the London Film Critics Awards, where he was in the running for a prize, to avoid an encounter with Nicole. Friends confirmed that no such liaison had taken place, but that Nicole had simply been a shoulder to cry on for the troubled star. She later gave credence to these comments when reporters cornered her at the British premiere of *The Hours* by saying, 'I think we need to respect their privacy. It's not true but I don't think it's right for me to say anything more.'

Shortly after, Jude issued the following statement: 'There is absolutely no third party involved in our marriage. To suggest otherwise is malicious, hurtful and libellous.' He went on to say, 'While we truly appreciate the concern the media has shown towards us, we ask that you now please give us the privacy we eagerly need so that we can put our lives in order.' When quizzed about the reports, Sadie dismissed them as 'a load of rubbish'. She added, 'We are trying to get our family back together after all these stupid lies... People just put two and two together and get five. We want to spend time with our children.'

But by now Jude and Sadie's unstable marriage was a hot headline topic. By November, the media intrusion had become so bad that the couple decided to move house. While choosing to remain in the Primrose Hill area, they were after a place with better security. Attempts to photograph his kids had infuriated Jude. 'The attention from the paparazzi is like being followed by snipers,' he told pals. 'It's worse than ever now: they're actually asking for pictures of my kids.'

But a new home did little to alleviate the problems. Reports filtered through that police had been called out twice to the couple's home after reports of a disturbance. Jude played down the rumours, condemning unscrupulous police officers for selling stories to the press. 'There were two instances where the police were called for whatever reason to my old house and the story was sold, telling lies,' he told the *Guardian* newspaper. 'The police were responding to phone calls that happened, but they were then coming out and creating an atmosphere, a drama, when actually nothing had happened; there were no charges pressed. But then there's selling stories, so how are you going to live in a country and feel safe?' Now following the couple's every move, paparazzi photographers managed to snap a tearful Sadie wheeling her buggy in the rain. It was the shot they'd been after.

While close friends of Sadie and Jude insisted their marriage was 'solid', it was obvious all was not well. The family took an extended break to Thailand over Christmas to try to patch things up.

In January 2003, the relationship hit rock bottom when it was alleged 37-year-old Sadie had become suicidal and tried to slit her wrists in a bid for attention. Her best friend and business partner, Jemima French, dismissed the stories as complete fabrication. After joining Jude in America for the Golden Globe Awards, Sadie flew home alone. Sadie's spokeswoman Mina Kherahas told the press, 'There have been problems with their marriage. This is mainly due to the fact that they hardly spent any time at all with each other last year. Jude was always away working while Sadie was at home looking after four children and this has put a bit of strain on them. But they do both want to try to make it work and things have been a lot healthier since they had a holiday.' Under the auspices of their Natural Nylon venture, the couple were also due to start work on a new film, *Sky Captain and the World of Tomorrow*, a sci-fi story set in 1939 starring Jude alongside Gwyneth Paltrow. 'Working on a film together is just what they need as they will be able to spend time with each other,' Sadie's spokeswoman insisted. They would also be acting alongside each other in *Psychoville*, a suburban gothic thriller they'd been developing for five years. After discharging herself from a clinic, Sadie later said, 'I'm feeling fantastic at the moment. It was just post-natal depression. There are no marriage problems.'

Indeed, no sooner had the suicide rumours subsided than Jude announced his wife was suffering from 'severe' post-natal depression and had checked herself into a private London clinic. After receiving a troubled phone call from Sadie, he jumped straight on the next plane to be by her side. In a public statement, he revealed, 'When Sadie arrived back in England at the weekend she went straight into a clinic. She has been suffering a severe bout of post-natal depression.' But he insisted her treatment would not involve taking drugs, 'just seeing doctors, talking and recuperating. She is there because she is feeling very blue.' He added, 'This depression can be a serious thing and it has left Sadie feeling very sad and run-down and she is just trying to get a handle on it. She has had so much on her plate recently and realises she needs help and to catch her breath. Not only does she have to look after four children – including a baby – she runs a successful business and has been overseeing the refurbishment of our new house.' But, in the same breath, Jude shrugged off suggestions Sadie would be in the clinic for any longer than a couple of days.

Just two weeks later, however, Jude had moved back to the family's old home, leaving Sadie and the kids in their new property. Whispers suggested the couple had split up, but were waiting for the media attention to die down before they announced anything. Fanning the gossip flames even further, Sadie appeared on a BBC3 documentary and cryptically spoke of her fears about becoming a single mother: 'My own parents split up three times. I would find it terrifying that I would have to go through being a single parent. It would be such a heart wrench for me if my marriage didn't work out,' she shuddered, before quickly adding, '[but] it is so important that you don't stay with someone just for the children and for the wrong reasons.' Once again, Jude and Sadie planned a holiday to help patch up their differences. Leaving the kids at home, they set off for a weekend in Oxfordshire, where they did nothing but 'eating, sleeping and making love'.

The reunion was short-lived, however, and soon the

couple found themselves involved in a very acrimonious split. Initially, Sadie convinced herself the break-up was only temporary. She complained that her marriage problems had 'been blown out of all proportion', although she agreed she and Jude needed to 'sort things out'. But, when the couple met up in June to discuss their marriage, negotiations very quickly erupted into argument. Their choice of neutral venue, a local pub, was hardly appropriate. With children in tow, the couple had difficulty keeping their voices down as a bitter row ensued. According to bystanders, Sadie was taking digs at Jude through talking to the children, saying, 'Mummy gets very bored and lonely sitting at home every night.' Jude reportedly had a face like thunder.

The break-up caused major ructions not only for the couple, but also within the couple's trendy Primrose Hill set. Both sides had their supporters and the close-knit clan was quickly divided in two. Among Sadie's supporters were Stella McCartney and Kate Moss, while Jude could count on the allegiance of Ewan McGregor, Gwyneth Paltrow and Sean Pertwee. 'Sadie and Jude have managed to completely divide up a really tight-knit bunch of friends – who also happen to be among the most famous stars in the world,' said one insider. 'It's not like everybody can be friends with everyone, and people have strong opinions about the split.

'Jude has found himself totally cold-shouldered by one bunch, and Sadie has been snubbed by people like

Gwyneth, who she used to consider a friend. The bitterness between them is so strong. You just can't be seen to be friends with both.' This caused major problems for couples like Kate Moss and Jefferson Hack and Sadie's sister Holly, whose boyfriend was still Jude's best friend and PR.

Reasons for the split remained vague. So many factors had hampered the marriage that it was difficult to discern exactly what had been the final straw. Some friends claimed Jude was simply fed up with Sadie's theatrical antics; others cruelly suggested that she'd become a millstone around his neck and was hampering any advance in his Hollywood career. It was also suggested Jude was simply fed up with trying to ingratiate himself with Sadie's new fashion buddies. Later, Sadie would even apportion most of the blame to herself: 'I think maybe it put me under a lot of stress having the babies so close together,' she reflected. When Sadie eventually filed for divorce, after six years of marriage, she cited Jude's 'unreasonable behaviour'. But the real motivation remained unclear. Eighteen months later in January 2005, various newspapers came up with a very probable explanation. Supergrass drummer Danny Goffey and his girlfriend Pearl Lowe had been good friends with Jude and Sadie for quite some time. But, when tales of their salacious relationship were printed in a Sunday paper, no one was quite prepared for the revelations in store.

According to an unnamed source, the foursome had regularly indulged in partner swapping. The controlled infidelity had allegedly started in the summer of 2001 when the group were on holiday in Greece. 'Pearl and Danny were having a brilliant time with Jude and Sadie at their villa in Greece,' the paper stated. According to the report, the couple continued to swap partners when they returned back home to London and Jude became increasingly fascinated by Pearl. 'Jude would tell Pearl he thought she was wonderful and couldn't believe he was sleeping with her,' said the source. But, when Sadie discovered an email from Jude to Pearl suggesting they have a full-blown affair, the bed-hopping came to an abrupt end. 'She flew into a rage and smashed up the house before a remorseful Jude calmed her down,' the source continued. 'After that, things really changed and Jude and Pearl never made love again.' But just months later Jude and Sadie separated, even though they insisted a third party was never involved.

Understandably embarrassed by the reports, Jude and Sadie remained tight-lipped. But, to their horror, more stories started to surface. The *Daily Mirror* reported that *Notting Hill* star Rhys Ifans and his girlfriend at the time, Jess Morris, had turned down an offer from the couple to partake in their wife-swapping sessions. A friend was quoted as saying, 'Rhys is good pals with Sadie's crowd, but he couldn't believe what was going on. He's now split up with Jess, but he would never jeopardise a relationship like that.'

Then matters took a real downturn when Pearl Lowe confirmed to the *News of the World* that the stories were in fact true. She claimed the sessions had almost ruined her relationship with Danny Goffey: 'The story's correct – even though I wish it wasn't,' she said. 'I'd much rather be remembered as Pearl the Singer than Pearl the Swinger. It was a time in mine and Danny's lives that I would rather forget.' Speaking of the tumultuous aftermath, she said, 'Things got very difficult and tense between the four of us immediately after it all happened… I still talk to Sadie – she's a friend of mine. But Danny and I haven't spoken properly to Jude for ages.' Jude and Sadie refuted the allegations.

But all of this was revealed much later. At the time of Jude and Sadie's separation, no one was any the wiser. As far as they were concerned, British cinema's fairytale couple had met with a very unhappy ending. Even the tabloids carved up their allegiance – some criticising Sadie for her riotous and unkempt behaviour, while others ridiculed 'moody Judey' for being a po-faced misery. For everyone involved, the situation had escalated into a complete nightmare.

Then, into this furore walked a very naive and innocent Sienna Miller.

FIVE

Changing Partners

LIKE everyone else in the world, Sienna had been party to Jude's private life. Even before the couple had met, she knew more about him than a stranger really should. While Sienna's friends all agreed Jude was a catch, he was a catch who came with a lot of baggage. Sienna knew full well that having a relationship with a high-profile star like Jude Law wasn't going to be easy. But she didn't choose to fall in love with him. By all accounts, it was an inevitability she simply couldn't avoid.

Given Jude's delicate marital situation, the new loves initially chose to keep their relationship under wraps. But it didn't take long for the tabloids to pick up on the scent of romance. Sienna told reporters, 'It's inevitable that people imagine Jude and I are getting together because he's going through a divorce with Sadie Frost and I've broken up with my boyfriend. It's been a very exciting few weeks, but it's difficult to know what to say. You do fall a little bit in love with everyone you're working with on some artistic level. I'm convinced of it.' Some cynics even suggested the relationship was a stunt to boost box-office figures.

At first, Jude insisted the couple weren't photographed together – partly out of respect for his family but also out of concern any unwelcome interventions might stifle the relationship before it had even been given a chance to develop. But neither Jude nor Sienna could contain their happiness for long. Very soon, pictures of the couple behaving like love-struck teenagers were splashed across newsstands. Whether it was spoon-feeding each other ice cream in New York, taking a stroll through the park or kissing passionately at a party, Jude and Sienna were very much an official item.

In spite of all the chaos around him, Jude felt calmer than he had in years. With Sienna, he'd found a soul mate. In contrast to his tempestuous relationship with Sadie, Sienna breezed into his life like a refreshing breath of fresh air. Jude's close friends couldn't help but remark on his new, relaxed demeanour. On several occasions, he was even photographed smiling – something he hadn't done for months.

When Jude's parents arrived to meet Sienna on the *Alfie*

set, they were delighted by his new choice of companion. 'She's simply wonderful,' commented his father. 'Well done, son.'

That morning Sienna confessed to being nervous about the encounter. Her feelings for Jude were extremely intense and she knew the relationship was more than a fleeting affair. The fact Jude was willing to introduce her to his parents was testimony in itself. She wanted them to like her and was anxious to make a good impression. As Sadie was the mother of Jude's three children, Sienna was convinced their sympathies would lie with her. By all accounts, Sienna was a rival. For all she knew, they could have been desperate for Jude and Sadie to have a reconciliation.

Sienna couldn't have been more wrong. As it turned out, they had a lot in common and never once stumbled for conversation. According to one source, Jude's parents had never really been fond of Sadie – they found her to be abrupt and difficult. Sienna, on the other hand, was just the type of girl they'd always dreamed Jude would bring home. She was friendly, polite, well educated and came from a good background.

Both Jude and Sienna had enjoyed a similar upbringing. Both were relatively well off, had attended expensive private schools and enjoyed a relatively stable family life. Neither was a rebel, a trailblazer or an outrageous extrovert. Indeed, Jude was secretly quite relieved to have met someone far removed from Sadie's trendy Primrose

Hill clique. He'd always felt quite uncomfortable around Sienna's fashion friends and had felt the need to cultivate an image that wasn't quite faithful to himself. In interviews, for instance, he always claimed his parents had named him after the Beatles classic 'Hey, Jude'. It later transpired, however, that his name had rather different origins – Thomas Hardy's *Jude The Obscure*.

More hardened cynics would also argue that, given Jude's credentials as a serious actor, calm Sienna was a far better complement than the wayward Sadie. Albeit not in the same league as Jude, the young star had a bright Hollywood career ahead of her. She had also recently topped *Tatler*'s prestigious 'Most Invited' list of Britain's most desirable party guests. Sadie, on the other hand, had failed to make the magazine's final 100. 'Both have the same aim in mind,' said an insider. 'He likes being part of a glamorous couple. He didn't end his relationship with Sadie to go rampaging from one woman to the next – he likes being married.'

Another big consideration for Sienna was Jude's children. At first, she was frightened they might resent Daddy's new girlfriend and see her as an intruder in the family. Equally, she was aware of how important Raff, Iris and Rudy were to Jude. He spoke about them constantly, always with a glint of happiness in his eye. On numerous occasions while out filming *Alfie* in New York, Jude had stopped off at various shops to buy gifts and trinkets for his kids. 'Right from the start, he told Sienna that the children were his priority. She knew she had no chance with him unless she got on with the kids,' reported one insider. Sienna found Jude's fatherly love endearing and added it to an already long list of virtuous qualities. She admired Jude for having given up his freedom to become a parent at such a young age. Despite being young herself, she wasn't at all fazed about the prospect of adopting a ready-made family as her own. In fact, she was eager to be accepted.

Jude was keen for Sienna to meet his children and was certain they would all get along. One afternoon, when it was his turn to look after them, he invited Sienna to take a trip with them to the park. She wanted the day to run perfectly and planned every activity in minute detail. She even asked Jude for a list of what the kids liked and didn't like. Were they allowed to drink Coca-Cola or Ribena? Would Rafferty eat fish fingers? She was determined to make a good impression.

When Sienna arrived at Jude's Primrose Hill house, she already had a day's worth of activities planned. First, she took the kids kite-flying, then they returned home to bake cakes. The children took to her instantly and by all accounts the meeting was a success. 'She did a real Mary Poppins number!' said one friend. Jude was delighted. He was touched by the amount of effort Sienna had gone to and recognised she had a real way with kids.

'They think you're fantastic,' he said, hugging her close to his chest.

'I hope so!' she replied.

Indeed, Sienna took to domesticity like a duck to water. She loved to stay home and look after the kids and was forever cooking dinner and cleaning the house whenever she had the opportunity. No sooner had she settled into her own flat than she wanted to help Jude build a new home. Even by her own admission, Sienna was a homely character. Sometimes, Rafferty would come in from football training covered in mud. 'Come here!' she would chastise him, jokingly, before stripping off his dirty clothes and putting them straight in the washing machine. She'd loved children and had always envisioned having a big family of her own. Even very early on, she counted having babies among her ambitions. When asked by a journalist about her long-term goals, she replied, 'Oh my God! I don't know! Probably with a few babies eventually, making a living out of what I like doing and being happy. I try not to think too far ahead because I could jinx things, but I'm trying to live for the moment. I suppose being happy and in love – I always want to be in love.'

'The children are fond of her,' said one friend. 'She's a very calm person to be around – although Sadie is still their mum.'

Some newspapers also cruelly claimed that Jude had been attracted to Sienna because of her subservience. Sadie had been the dominant force in his previous relationship, but now Jude was calling the shots. Sienna was painted as a forlorn and awe-struck puppy dog, hanging on Jude's every move. Of course, this was a gross exaggeration. Sienna certainly doted on Jude, but she was no insipid pushover.

The main difference seemed to be that Sienna was a lot more amenable than her stubborn and caustic forerunner. She very rarely made demands of Jude and always made his happiness a priority. 'She's a real people-pleaser,' commented one friend. Laid-back and carefree, Sienna sought to avoid complications. Sadie, however, seemed to court drama and conflict. When Jude flew to America to work on a new film, Sienna was in floods of tears. Allegedly, Jude called Sadie immediately to ask why she'd never behaved in a similar way! Sienna was the warm-hearted princess; Sadie the volatile ice maiden.

When Sadie first caught wind that Jude had a new girlfriend, her reaction was predictable. She sneered and dismissed the relationship as 'a silly fling'. Sadie, however, had a new love interest of her own. Only a day after she announced she was planning to divorce Jude, Sadie was pictured cavorting with her 23-year-old toyboy flamenco musician Jackson Scott. The pair were snapped sharing a bottle of wine in Regent's Park. Sadie seemed to make no attempts to be discreet. Flaunting her newly acquired freedom, she couldn't care less who saw them. Mutual friends of Sadie and Jude were appalled. It was rumoured that Gwyneth Paltrow was upset by Sadie's behaviour, and concerned by Sadie's apparent lack of concern for her estranged husband.

Jackson and Sadie had become acquainted a few weeks

earlier when Sadie was holidaying in Seville. Jackson's mother ran a guesthouse in the area; he had been brought up in Spain and Sadie was relieved to have found someone outside her set. 'It makes things interesting,' she told friends. Nor was she worried about the age gap: 'I think it's a good relationship for now,' she insisted. 'There are lots of examples of relationships with age gaps that do work.'

Onlookers commented on the spooky coincidence that Jude and Sadie had both taken on lovers of exactly the same age. In an even more bizarre twist of fate, it turned out that Sienna and Scott had actually been teenage sweethearts themselves. (Their families were friends.)

Even though Jude and Sadie had separated, they still had several important work commitments to honour. The film *Sky Captain and the World of Tomorrow*, which the pair had co-produced, was due for release. Both parties were expected at the premiere, but to ease any tensions they had both agreed to leave their respective lovers at home. When the evening came, however, not everything went to plan. While Jude dutifully obliged and turned up without Sienna, Sadie chose to ignore her promise, and waltzed down the red carpet with Jackson on her arm. One couldn't help but wonder whether it had all been a sly and calculated move to upstage Jude. The actor was furious.

It wasn't until Christmas that Sadie and Sienna officially met. By that time, Jude was serious about Sienna and was anxious for the women to acquaint themselves, if only for the children's sake. Sienna was about to become a permanent fixture in his life, so Sadie had better get used to it. Sienna was terrified. Her hands were shaking as she gripped her glass of champagne tightly. Much older and more confident than the young star, Sadie was a formidable character. She was also armed with an acerbic tongue and wasn't afraid to use it. On meeting Sienna, Sadie realised just how vulnerable and nervous the younger woman really was. Fawn-like, she cowered timidly in the shadows. Despite the odd scathing comment to the press, Sadie wasn't a dragon. She didn't want to make the young girl feel uncomfortable. She took Jude to one side and told him she approved. The three agreed that the children would spend mornings with Sadie and afternoons with Jude and Sienna.

Sadie and Sienna's relationship was further cemented when the pair bumped into each other at the Glastonbury festival in Somerset the following summer. On this occasion, Sienna was without Jude and was enjoying the famous music festival with friends. Being a rock'n'roll chick at heart, Sadie was something of a regular face at the event. Usually she could be found with her best pal Kate Moss in tow. Backstage at the celebrity beer tent, Sadie noticed Sienna huddled in the corner with friends. Wanting to declare their friendship publicly, she waltzed over and bestowed a hug on the somewhat surprised actress. The public act of affection was photographed and made tabloid headlines the following day. When asked about the embrace, Sienna replied, 'She is the mother of my boyfriend's kids and a wonderful woman.'

According to insiders, Sadie was sick and tired of people assuming she didn't like Sienna. As far as she was concerned, the meek and young elfin-like creature was harmless. She also knew how highly her children regarded Jude's new girlfriend. Rafferty, in particular, was anxious that Sienna, Sadie, Jude and Jackson should all get along. Sadie's children were her priority and their happiness was paramount. At first Sienna perhaps wasn't sure how to interpret the gesture. She was in no doubt that Sadie's intentions were genuine, but her sudden wave of emotion could have made Sienna feel a little nervous and uncomfortable. She was already quite intimidated by Jude's ex. 'She appears confident, but she's scared rigid of Sadie,' said an insider. 'She absolutely wouldn't want to get into a fight with Sadie. She's just not that sort of person, and Jude would hate it as well.' And so the two formed an amicable, but slightly awkward, friendship.

Unfortunately, not all of Sadie's relationships were faring so well. While things were improving between herself and Sienna, relations with Jude had plummeted to an all-time low. The couple now found themselves embroiled in a messy divorce battle, played out daily in the press. The affidavit from the decree nisi was even sent directly from the High Court to a tabloid newspaper before it eventually reached Jude. It seemed a predictable end to a marriage apparently plagued by conflict and trauma. Originally, both parties had agreed to make the divorce as smooth as possible for the sake of their children. When the couple first announced their intentions publicly, Sadie issued a statement to the press: 'We have agreed that a divorce is the only way forward but we have equally agreed that we will do everything in our power to make certain that this is as painless a process as possible for the benefit of the children. They are our number-one priority and have always been so and will remain so.'

But any chances of a swift resolution quickly disappeared. For almost a year, the couple haggled over a final settlement. Reportedly, Sadie wanted the family home in Belsize Park (worth £2.7 million), a lump sum and in excess of £25,000 a month. As Jude could earn up to £5 million a film, she felt it was her due.

Both Sadie and Jude refused to budge and spent enormous sums of money on legal advice and manoeuvrings. 'The legal thing with those two is lunacy!' said one friend. Unhappy with the way things were going, Jude even ditched his legal team halfway through proceedings. 'I wouldn't be surprised if he's spent a six-figure sum on lawyers already and now he's starting again,' said another source. Allegedly, Sadie was keeping a detailed diary of her rows with Jude. There were even rumours she'd taped Jude shouting down the phone at her.

Herself a mild-mannered character, Sienna hated argument and confrontation. Her own parents' divorce had been a breeze in comparison to Jude and Sadie's fraught negotiations. She even went so far as to discuss the situation with Sadie, to see if a compromise could be reached. But, when Jude found out she'd interfered, he was furious. The couple were out to dinner in a London restaurant when Sienna broached the topic. She begged Jude to end his bitter divorce battle and reach a compromise with Sadie. Jude refused to listen and the two ended up in an argument. 'Sienna just wants to move on,' said a friend. 'She is absolutely love-struck and had no idea Jude would react the way he did.'

It was hard not to pity Sadie. She'd been through a lot in the past few months: she'd suffered post-natal depression, separated from Jude, and lost her father, an alcoholic with whom she shared a troubled relationship, to liver disease. Now her life seemed even more complicated than ever before. Soon after her split with Jude, she was commissioned by Channel 4 to present her own TV show. *What Sadie Did Next* would be broadcast on the channel's satellite arm, E4. The actress apparently impressed bosses after taking part in a *100 Greatest Musicals* special to be broadcast that Christmas. They intended to model the show in the vein of 1980s music show *The Tube*, which was hosted by Jools Holland and Paula Yates. It was hoped Sadie would use her contacts to pull in an army of A-list stars, but according to reports in the *Sun* newspaper – aside from Gwyneth Paltrow – she'd failed to attract any major stars. Subsequently, the show was dropped and Sadie's aspirations as a TV presenter met with an abrupt end. Bosses at the channel said, 'The show was only ever commissioned for one series. It will appear again with a different presenter.'

Sadie's wild and untempered social life was also the topic of much tabloid speculation. On several occasions, she had vowed to curb her drunken behaviour, but she was constantly seen out on the town looking 'tired and emotional'. She was snapped sozzled following her FrostFrench fashion show after-party and, after leaving a bash at London celebrity haunt the Met Bar, was oblivious to the trickle of sick down her top. 'Sadie was in a right state that night,' said a source. 'Later, she got in an argument with Davinia Taylor [ex-*Hollyoaks* actress and party girl], obviously fuelled by booze.' The worst occasion was Kate Moss's 30th birthday party in January 2004.

Kate was a notorious wild child with a phonebook that read like a Who's Who of the celebrity world. As a result, her parties were always a highlight on the celebrity social calendar, with everyone from supermodels to rock stars vying for an invitation. Those on the guest list included Jade Jagger, Grace Jones, Gwyneth Paltrow, Chris Martin, Tracey Emin, Alexander McQueen and Stella McCartney. Kate wasn't about to let her 30th go by unnoticed and, true to her reputation, she threw a riotous bash. The party took place in a suite at the grandiose marble-clad and chandelier-strewn Claridges hotel and was themed 'The Beautiful and The Damned'. Kate asked her guests to dress in 1920s style and arrived herself in a sparkling evening dress, her hair curled in ringlets. As expected, the party quickly descended into debauchery and it was claimed that a wild orgy took place. The *News of the World* even alleged a lesbian threesome had taken place between Kate, Sadie and Davinia: 'Kate was high and the other two were drunk at a bash. They went up to a suite and got in bed together,' a source told the paper. 'Kate started chatting about sex. She asked Davinia if she'd ever done it with a woman before and that was it.'

Fashion PA Rebecca White, who has known the catwalk beauty since 1998, revealed, 'Kate is naturally a very sexually open person. But, when she's doing cocaine, she becomes even more so and will fall into bed with whoever she chooses. Women as well as men.'

The report went on to suggest that this wasn't the first sexual encounter between Kate and Sadie. Apparently, it had become something of a regular pastime between the two friends. 'Sadie doesn't really fancy other women, but it has become normal between her and Kate,' said a source. 'At one of Kate's parties, Sadie was having sex openly with Kate and they were all over each other's breasts.' Reportedly, Jude had become jealous of their intimacy and started to resent Sadie being alone with Kate. Supposedly, the pair then invited Jude to join in so he wouldn't feel left out.

Of course, Jude denied these rumours. He was even more horrified to open the papers the morning after Kate's 30th and find humiliating pictures of his ex-wife drunk. At one point, she'd been so trolleyed that one of her boobs had fallen out of her dress. Jude was appalled. It wasn't the sort of behaviour you'd expect from a mother of four.

Sadie would later hit back at the tabloids, vehemently denying any claims that she was an unsuitable mother. 'To tell you the truth, I'm the kind of person who'll have a few drinks and fall asleep at eleven,' she insisted, somewhat unconvincingly. 'I'm such a lightweight. When I have a couple of drinks, I become quite extrovert, but that doesn't mean I'm wild or do any of the things people say. I went to stage school. I put my tap shoes on. I perform. When I go out with friends, I don't just sit there. I jump around. I don't see anything wrong with that. But I don't crawl in at six in the morning, ever.' She went on to argue that two very public occasions on which she had been drunk were connected to the death of her father. 'I'd had three drinks; it is to do with emotions, hormones, that sort of thing.'

The whole Jude and Sadie affair had become something of a soap opera and merited priority inches in the daily gossip columns. It was inevitable that Sienna would soon be swept up into their complicated world. For the time being, she didn't mind. Although, eventually, the media circus that seemed to surround Jude would put an unbearable pressure on her own relationship with the actor. But for now, even in the face of the greatest adversities, Sienna was the happiest woman alive. Irrespective of what was going on around her, she had Jude. That was all that mattered.

SIX

Sienna the Style-setter

Boho-chic: a style of female fashion (c.2003–05) associated particularly with the actress Sienna Miller (b.1981).

(Source: Wikipedia)

FIRST coined in the early 20th century, the word 'bohemian' was originally used to describe travellers and refugees from central Europe, otherwise referred to as gypsies. The word was later adopted by the literary Bloomsbury set and used to describe a lifestyle that existed outside the normal parameters of society. Generally, this was the realm of artists and creative types. Bohemian fashion traits at that time included bobbed hair and full, brightly coloured skirts. Later, the term became synonymous with members of America's beat generation of the 1950s.

By 2002 the 'boho' look was back in vogue. The style was first associated with Kate Moss, with magazines referring to certain looks as 'very cool, very bohemian, very Kate Moss-y'. Kaftans, leather belts and gypsy skirts quickly appeared on the catwalk. However, it was Sienna who effortlessly breezed the look into mainstream fashion. Indeed, her W10 postal code (North Kensington) had been associated with the style since the 1950s.

Fashion editors hailed Sienna as a style icon. They praised the actress for her distinctive and on-point dress sense. She would pair up unusual items but effortlessly carry off an outfit that might look ridiculous on anyone else. On several occasions, she was photographed wearing furry gilets, large belts and sheepskin Ugg boots. Sienna also had a tendency to mix and match her price range, teaming labels such as Missoni with bargain vintage items from Portobello Road market. 'I'm into Marc Jacobs, but I also like market stuff, vintage Vivienne Westwood and little prairie tops that you can find for a tenner at Portobello.'

Other stars were quick to follow Sienna's lead and the high street inevitably followed suit. Soon it was impossible to walk around the Notting Hill area without bumping into a Sienna Miller clone. Even internet auction site eBay started listing clothing products as 'very Sienna'. Marks & Spencer launched their spring/summer collection in honour of the actress, while New Look reported sales of three million ponchos after Sienna had been snapped wearing a designer version. Cheaper versions of Sienna's staple £800 Chloé handbag were also flooding the market.

Sienna radiated beauty when she attended the Möet and Chandon tribute to her good friend Matthew Williamson at London Fashion Week, February 2005.

Before Sienna hit the silver screen.

Above left: Being interviewed by Carson Daley on the American chat show *Last Call*, June 2003.

Above right: Sienna's first TV acting break came when she breezed her audition for the part of Fiona in a new American TV police drama called *Keen Eddie*.

Below: Sienna on screen with Daniel Craig in the film *Layer Cake*. Although Sienna only had a minor role, her film debut lived up to all of her expectations – it gave her the chance to perform alongside Daniel Craig and Michael Gambon, two of her idols.

Sienna nervously lapping up the celebrity treatment backstage at Carson Daley's *Last Call* with her then boyfriend, David Neville. Little did she know that almost overnight she would shoot to fully-fledged stardom and this luxurious treatment would become the norm for her.

Above: Sienna on screen with Jude Law in the new version of *Alfie*. Everyone involved in the film agreed that there was an immediate spark between Jude and Sienna off screen as well as on, and before the filming was finished the pair were an item.

Below left: Jude with his ex-wife Sadie Frost.

Below right: Sienna and Jude received an incredible reception when they attended the world premiere of *Alfie* in London, October 2004. Despite the terrible weather, the fans turned out in their thousands to catch a glimpse of the recently announced couple.

Above left: Sienna fooling around with her new pal Mick Jagger and looking totally at home on the red carpet.

Above right: Sienna with Josephine Miller, her very proud mother.

Below: The whole family turned out to witness Sienna's first major film premiere. From left to right: Savannah Miller, Josephine Miller, Ed Miller, and Ed's partner June.

Sienna and Jude's romance was splashed across all the tabloids. Wherever they went they were photographed.

Above: The pair were unable escape the cameras as they tried to enjoy some quality time together at the Wimbledon quarter final, but it was evident that no amount of unwanted attention could dampen Sienna's happiness.

Below left: The happy couple relaxing on their holiday in Mexico, still unable to avoid the tabloid photographers.

Below right: Jude ambling in Primrose Hill with his and Sienna's two terriers, Porgy and Bess.

Photographers did not only hound Sienna because of her relationship with Jude Law, she quickly carved out her own niche in the celebrity market. She became a huge style icon in the UK. This is the infamous front-page photo of Sienna at Glastonbury, which apparently stole a bit of Kate Moss's festival limelight.

In the public's eye, in 2002 Sienna began to take over Kate Moss's reign as the queen of style. Her distinctive boho dress sense quickly became the inspiration for mainstream fashion trends. She was considered such an icon that she couldn't even go to the shops or walk her dogs without a photograph of her appearing in one of the glossy magazines.

Although flattered by all the attention, Sienna was slightly disgruntled to see her distinguished look become a supermarket-shelf commodity. As much as she hated her style being scrutinised, she despised it being copied. 'I've always liked nice clothes, and suddenly these beautiful vintage clothes that I've collected in the weirdest shops in the world are copied for a tenner in Topshop, which drives me mad. There's a perfect copy or a bit nicer, because they've added a bow.'

When dressing Sienna for the Venice Film Festival, fashion designer Roland Mouret said of the actress, 'Sienna is what happens every decade in London; this real new person that represents a generation. She has all the ingredients of what a British girl is about in the twenty-first century: she's from a nice family but down-to-earth, is incredibly charismatic but doesn't believe it, and has this idea of quality... She's not playing the game. She's just being herself.'

Sienna had never set out to create an image. Nothing about her appearance was contrived. 'I don't try to project any kind of public persona. If I try to calculate, then it all starts going wrong in my head. I lead a very boring life. If I started to dress for anyone else, or trim myself today, it would just screw my head up.' More than anything, Sienna dressed for herself. She had never been a follower of fashion. Instead, she found inspiration in more obscure places. 'I don't dress for anybody but myself. I see it as self-expression. It's inspired by places I've been or art or music:

Keith Richards, the beatniks. But I'm not trying to make it sound profound – I get it really horribly wrong at times.'

'I love clothes, but I'm not particularly fashion conscious. I collect clothes. I love the kind of history behind who has worn them before. I know what I like to wear and I'm a girl and I enjoy shopping. But I don't like to look too ostentatious or too glamorous; I'm a bit scruffy…' Jokingly, she added, 'It's just an item of clothing. I'm much happier naked!'

Sienna took a humble stance on her newfound fashion status. As far as she was concerned, she was simply dressing the way she wanted. In fact, she found all the attention quite amusing. If only these so-called fashion editors knew how lazy she really was! Quite often, she'd leave the house with tousled hair and unshaven legs. What in the past would be considered uncouth had now become a fashionable look, it seemed! She credited the UK for championing this new laid-back style. 'I think English people have a tendency not to be so done up and indulgent. In America, you can go and have a pedicure for ten dollars on the side of the street and everyone's kind of preened but in England it's fifty quid. Fuck that! So we slob around and I love it. It's completely scruff but if there's a non-attachment to the way that you dress then it's always fantastic. As soon as people are designered up to the max, it shows and it's ostentatious.'

For the most part, Sienna preferred to ignore all the hype. The last thing she needed was a wardrobe panic every time she left the house. She just wanted to carry on as normal. 'I still go out in my pyjamas,' she joked. Besides, she hadn't always been that stylish. Had the fashion police encountered Sienna ten years ago, she would definitely have been up for arrest. 'I used to be mental when I was younger,' she told journalists, relishing their reaction. 'I had pink-and-white hair and had this big papier-mâché seahorse that rattled around my neck. I wore multi-coloured long skirts and scarves and beads.'

Fashion designers were desperate for some association with Sienna. Once she was seen sporting their goods, an upsurge in sales would shortly follow. Every young girl wanted to look like Miss Miller. Every week carloads of dresses, bags, coats, hats, make-up and body products would arrive on Sienna's doorstep. In a month, she might receive up to 26 handbags worth between £2,000 and £30,000 each. Sienna loved all the free gifts – she was certainly very spoiled! 'That's the one bonus,' she enthused. 'Fuck everything else. Free handbags!' Often she would invite friends over to her flat to take their pick of cast-offs.

Fashion editors, meanwhile, were eager to unlock the secrets to Sienna's style. How did she do it? Often, during interviews, they would accompany Sienna on a shopping trip. On one occasion, *US Vogue* took Sienna to visit New York-based designers Jack McCollough and Lazaro Hernandez, creators of the trendy Proenza Schouler label. The trio had lots in common and became instant friends. Eager to show off their latest designs, the Parson's School graduates gave Sienna free rein at their exclusive boutique. Showing a complete lack of inhibition, she stripped off, stopping only to apologise for 'flashing her stretch-marked ass'. She loved their mid-calf lengths and smock tops.

Later that afternoon, Sienna gave one poor shopkeeper the shock of her life when she arrived unannounced at a vintage clothes store.

'Can I have a few minutes?' she begged.

'Are you OK?' asked Sienna.

'I'm just so honoured to have you here!' the shopkeeper replied, blushing furiously.

Half an hour later, Sienna returned to pick out some items. Her eye fell on a tacky fake Versace belt. 'It's gotta be done!' she said, reaching for the offensive item. She then switched her attention to a straw and leopard-print belt. 'It's more Eighties than me; I think it will be fun.' Other items in her basket included a slinky black jersey halter evening dress, a beaded black Fifties V-neck shell, and a pair of thigh-high, zip-crossed suede boots with sections of fuchsia, yellow, orange and red.

Similar scenarios took place back in the UK. On a shopping trip to vintage clothes store OG2 on Portobello Road, Sienna managed to seek out the most extraordinary items on offer. Shopkeeper Duro Olowu remarked on her incredible ability to transform the 'unwearable' into next season's must-have item. She tried on a vintage rubber coat by Cristobal Balenciaga, but decided against it at the very last minute. Instead, she spied a Versace-style red-and-gold belt, which she tightened just below her chest. Her knack for wearing accessories in unusual ways has become her style signature. She would wear glass bangles pushed up over her elbows, or an African necklace slung across her shoulders like a military belt.

During interviews, Sienna was more than happy to swap style tips and recommend good shopping haunts in London. 'I quite like Matches,' she mused. 'The last thing I bought there was Marc Jacobs boots. Then there's Browns… they have really good buyers.' Another favourite store was Euforia: 'I quite like the Hoxton, Japanesey-style clothes.'

There were even rumours Sienna would start her own fashion line. After all, her sister Savannah was a fashion-design graduate from London's Central St Martins. Sienna and Jude had both attended her end-of-year fashion show. Virtually unnoticed, they climbed the steps of York Hall in Bethnal Green in drizzling rain. The venue had once been a boxing hall where the likes of Chris Eubank, Nigel Benn and Lennox Lewis had fought. For once, the paparazzi hadn't caught a whiff of the couple's whereabouts. It was a low-key affair, and Sienna loved it.

Savannah's first collection was a mix of silk, Spandex and lace, in shades of fluorescent yellow, flesh-beige and icy-grey. Called Bite Me, the line was inspired by a nightmare Savannah had in which a girl, trapped in a cage, was attacked by sharks and tigers. 'It expresses the pressure of being in the spotlight, in the public eye,' Savannah told friends. 'The tigers and sharks are shredding the girl's clothes with their teeth and fangs, which gave me the idea of distressing the fabrics and destroying them in a beautiful sense.' Elsewhere, her collection showed the influence of poets, peasants and circus clowns.

Afterwards, Jude commented, 'It was quite extraordinary. I was amazed at the diversity of talent. It was an eye-opener.'

Blown away by her sister's talent, Sienna felt extremely proud. She'd always known Savannah would grow up to have a career in fashion. She was forever making clothes. Even at the age of 12, she was making fancy-dress costumes out of bubble-pack and wire. Now Savannah planned to launch her own line. 'I'm starting off from a room in my mother's house in Fulham. But I have a potential backer and a business partner. I'm determined to succeed.' However, contrary to reports, Sienna was not planning to join her.

Sienna and Savannah had always shared a similar taste in clothes and would quite often swap items in their wardrobes. 'We raid each other's wardrobes sporadically, but not so much any more because we live at opposite sides of the world mostly,' Savannah told one magazine. 'We share an aesthetic and appreciate the same things. Unfortunately, I'm a little bigger so her clothes don't always fit.' Savannah also felt less pressure to look good on a daily basis. Living in the countryside, she would often wear simple jumpers and jeans. In fact, the most expensive item she owned was a £2,000 Balenciaga leather bomber jacket, purchased for £700 in a sale. 'I called my bank and begged them to lend me the money,' she confesses. 'I made up some hideous story about why I needed the cash urgently and was so chuffed when the sale went through.' But Savannah wasn't always low-maintenance. She would always dress up for business trips to London. 'My favourite piece is a knitted pencil skirt with a godet [panel to make the skirt flare] at the back. It's really nice when you wear your own stuff and people ask where you bought it, and you can say, "I made it."'

Although Sienna was keen to support her sister, she was generally shy of endorsing any beauty or fashion products. When quizzed about a potential cosmetics deal, she screwed up her nose and replied, 'I don't think I'd do it. The idea of suddenly appearing on TV and saying because I'm worth it would just make me sick. All these actors are doing fashion things and I'm thinking, Are you an actress of a model?' After a moment's hesitation, however, she added, 'I want to not do it, but I think if I was offered enough money I might change my mind.'

One label she did make an exception for was fair-trade clothing company People Tree, set up to sell covetable and sustainable clothing. Entrepreneur Safia Minney launched the company in Tokyo in the early 1990s with a view to helping people in the Third World earn a living. Many of the clothes were handmade by artisans. When Safia approached Sienna to model their latest collection, she was more than happy to help out. 'There's no reason why organic and fair-trade clothing can't be sexy,' said Sienna. 'I think fair-trade is going to be a huge influence on fashion.

The clothes are great, you know where they come from, and you can be confident that people haven't been exploited to make them. You can pay hundreds of pounds for a designer dress and not know what it cost the planet and some of its poorest people to produce. When you look behind the glossy surface you see suffering and exploitation; people are working for very low wages. I have been just as guilty as the next person in not wanting to think about this.'

The fashion shoot took place at the Painswick Rococo Gardens in the Cotswolds. Sienna selected her outfits carefully. A velour skirt was pulled up around her breasts to make a dress, while an alpaca scarf was worn as a bandeau top. 'The clothes definitely make you feel earthy, feminine and sexy,' she commented. But, more than the clothes themselves, Sienna strongly believed in the ethical issues behind the project. 'By choosing to buy organic clothes, you can look good and feel great, and you're giving something back. I think that everyone should do their bit. I'm becoming more aware of the ways in which our food and clothes are produced. I try to buy organic food and I want to avoid genetically modified ingredients. We can all make a difference, even if it's just choosing to buy organic knickers instead of designer-label ones. You are using your consumer power to make a choice, and that helps to raise awareness.'

Up until Sienna had appeared on the scene, Kate Moss had been the leading light in UK fashion. Both she and Sienna shared a similar sense of style, so it was inevitable the pair would be pitted against each other in competition. The fact that Kate also happened to be best mates with Jude's ex-wife Sadie Frost only exacerbated the supposed rivalry. For the most part, Sienna found any comparison embarrassing. She'd hate people to think that she'd piggy-backed on someone else's style. 'Oh, God, no!' she replied to one interviewer at the very suggestion she and Kate shared similar rail space, though she went on to admit, 'She's got fantastic style, so I suppose I'd be stupid not to be flattered.'

When the broadsheets chose to use Sienna in place of Kate as their obligatory front-page Glastonbury shot, it seemed war had been declared. Wearing oversized yellow sunglasses and a short skirt, Sienna stole the show. 'My mum loved that shot!' she later giggled. 'Oh my darling!' she gasped, mimicking her mother's voice.

Kate, however, was less amused. 'The whole thing about her looking like Kate Moss is really funny,' claimed one insider. 'It does annoy Kate. She thinks Sienna copies her style.' On one occasion, Kate was reportedly fuming after Sienna was seen wearing a pair of black Birkenstock sandals only days after she'd worn them herself. She accused Sienna of working through her clothing back catalogue and decided to distance herself from the whole boho-chic look.

Even tempestuous supermodel Naomi Campbell came out in support of her friend, branding Sienna a cheap caricature of the catwalk queen. 'A lot of people compare the actress Sienna Miller to her. But I can't stand to hear that. I don't know Sienna Miller but there is no comparison to Kate. I don't like imitations, I like the real thing.' More stars follow suit. Actress Lindsay Lohan pledged her allegiance to Kate: 'Kate was there first,' she said simply, with a shrug.

The battle lines became more acutely obvious when Kate was dropped from her Burberry modelling campaign and Sienna was suggested as a replacement. The shamed super-waif was ousted following the publication of photographs seeming to show Kate snorting cocaine at a recording studio with her troubled musician boyfriend Pete Doherty. (Unknown to Kate, she had been filmed by someone with a mobile phone.) The newspaper reported that the video showed Kate doing five lines of coke in 40 minutes. Kate checked herself into a rehabilitation clinic. While several of her clients agreed to forgive the remorseful model, others chose to drop her from their campaigns.

'Sienna Miller is one name being discussed,' confirmed a representative from Burberry. Apparently, photographer Mario Testino, who was due to shoot Kate for the label's spring campaign, was furious that his friend had been dropped. Burberry feared he might quit and had called for emergency talks to discuss a replacement model. 'Yes, Mario and I are going to meet next week to discuss the campaign. But I'm afraid I can't tell you any more,' director Christopher Bailey told the press.

The contract never actually transpired, but that didn't

stop Kate from continuing her digs. She was overheard criticising the actress at the Ritz in Paris. 'Kate and her friends were pretty loud and not very discreet,' reported an observer. 'Someone mentioned Sienna and the rumours that she has split with Jude. The whole gang burst out laughing. Kate made a catty remark about how Sienna didn't deserve to be gracing the covers of so many magazines. She added that she hoped that, after splitting with Jude, Sienna would not be hanging around with her set any more.' Allegedly, the supermodel continued to complain that Sienna wasn't a model and she should just stick to making films.

However, Burberry's Christopher Bailey rubbished rumours that Kate Moss and Sienna Miller were feuding. He told *Grazia* magazine, 'Kate and Sienna just happen to be the most stylish women in Britain – along with Stella Tennant. Their style is completely different. Kate is very rock'n'roll and Sienna is incredibly eclectic. We dress them both.' He went on to suggest that, contrary to popular belief, the two women were actually good friends.

To call Kate and Sienna best pals would be a long shot at best, but by now they had at least both reached an understanding. Although they hailed from different worlds and backgrounds, they certainly had one thing in common – a dislike and distrust of the press. Sienna had never asked to be a fashion icon. In many ways, it detracted from her ultimate goal of achieving acting success. From now on, fashion would need to take a back seat. But the style press weren't about to let Sienna go that easily! Try as she might, there was no relinquishing the fashion mantle she'd haphazardly acquired. Every woman in the country was hanging on her every wardrobe move. Each time Sienna stepped out of the front door, she made a statement – even if that statement was 'leave me alone'. Sienna Miller had become a taste-maker – whether she liked it or not.

SEVEN

The Price of Fame

THE front desk of New York's Mercer Hotel was particularly busy that morning. Sipping thoughtfully on a glass of ice-cold Pellegrino, Sienna wondered if there was anything special going on in town that weekend. Jude had agreed to meet her in the lobby 20 minutes previously. She'd arisen early that morning for a newspaper interview; Jude, on the other hand, had chosen to stay in bed. Slightly weary herself from several late nights on the trot, she was jealous. But his tardiness didn't really bother her much; she was quite happy watching people waltz through the hotel's revolving doors.

It was a sunny morning and Sienna had chosen her outfit accordingly; a white Matthew Williamson dress, a vintage denim vest, dangly bracelets and cowboy boots.

Even though she still stubbornly refused to dress up for the press, being snapped in public was now a consideration. It was also a good opportunity to show off the imaginative outfits she'd rustled up at home.

'Hey, Sienna,' called out a gruff voice. It was Alfonso Curan, the director of *Harry Potter and the Prisoner of Azkaban*. He flashed a quick wave before disappearing into the hotel lifts.

Three minutes later, Gavin Rossdale, lead singer with Bush, breezed past. The pair exchanged pleasantries. 'Listen, do you and Jude fancy coming to see the show tonight?' he asked, in reference to his band's headline gig at Jonas Beach that night. 'Take my number,' he added, scribbling his mobile number down on a dog-eared piece of paper. 'Just give me a call.'

At that moment Jude appeared in shorts, T-shirt and a blazer – very much the Englishman in New York.

'What's happening?' said Gavin, extending his hand and nodding towards the *Time Out* guidebook to New York Jude is carrying.

'We're heading out to do some second-hand-book shopping,' Jude replied. 'Pamphlets, poetry, back issues, that kind of thing.'

'We're big fans,' Sienna quickly interjected, noticing the confused look on Gavin's face. 'I've got this group of friends that are quite bohemian and we get drunk, get the poetry books out and read. It sounds so pretentious but it's one of my favourite things.'

'Cool, well, maybe see you tonight,' replied Gavin, now slightly perplexed.

With that, Sienna and Jude disappeared through the hotel doors and into the blazing New York heat, joining another few thousand tourists on the sidewalk.

Straddling the world of celebrity and that of a normal couple was a practice Jude and Sienna made their own. As much as their lifestyle was a glamorous one, they also embraced the mundanity of everyday life. Sienna refused to believe that her life had really changed that much since she'd been catapulted to fame. 'I certainly wouldn't want to start obsessing about things because I think it would drive me insane. Jude and I are very normal people. We're actually very quiet. It's not like I sit there thinking, God, I'm dating someone who is very famous. You forget.'

In many ways, they had the ideal relationship; one night they might attend a cocktail party at the Met Bar or the Groucho Club, while the next they'd be out demonstrating against GM crops with fellow environmentalists. A champion of matters ethical, Sienna even vowed to lend her support and 'slash the crops' during a camping trip the two of them made to Tapeley Park in Devon.

Now convinced their relationship would last, the pair decided to move in together. Jude gave up his rented flat in Primrose Hill in exchange for a new property in Maida Vale. It was reported that both flats looked identical. But, to Sienna's relief, Jude was stepping away from his old life. A new house meant a new start. For now, Sienna was completely devoted to her boyfriend. His happiness took priority over everything else. 'I'm genuinely happy,' cooed Sienna. 'I'm not one of those people who think enough about things in my own life.'

A seven-ton lorry from the Scott's removal firm pulled up outside Jude and Sadie's £3-million marital home. Months earlier, Sadie and the children had moved to a house in Belsize Park. The original family home was now, however, at the centre of difficult divorce wranglings. The estranged couple had already made arrangements as to how their belongings should be divided. It hadn't been an easy task! Burly removal men were seen loading the truck with furniture, personal items and children's toys. Busy filming abroad, Jude had asked his brother to take care of the move, which cost in the region of £1,600. After several hours, the job was done and Jude's belongings were whisked off to his new pad 15 minutes up the road. A spokesperson confirmed the move: 'Jude has moved house today. Sienna continues to retain her own flat,' but she added, 'They are very much together.'

A two-storey Georgian property, Jude's new home was almost a carbon copy of his previous one. A spacious drive, protected by electronically controlled security gates, led up to the four-bedroom semi-detached house. Potted plants flanked the black front door, while high vaulted walls and a shady garden offered relative seclusion in the city centre. Jude and Sienna had fallen in love with the property straight away.

Amid Jude's plans to move, there were rumours a divorce

settlement had been reached with Sadie. Sadie's people denied that was the case. 'No final deal has been made yet and it's not imminent. Jude's just fired his legal team so that is going to slow things up a bit… Sadie is definitely going to stay put where she is in Belsize Park.'

Cohabitation suited Jude and Sienna well. They relished the opportunity to spend every minute of the day together. But they weren't alone. A lover of animals, Sienna insisted they adopt two pet dogs. Rather than go to an expensive breeder, Sienna preferred to adopt dogs from a rescue centre and contacted the Dogs in Need association forthwith. Organisers quickly hooked the couple up with two terriers, who had been rescued from a pound in Ireland. The delighted couple decided to name their two pets Porgy and Bess after the famous George Gershwin musical. 'They're rescue dogs,' she revealed. 'Little terrier mutts that were found in a dustbin in Ireland when they were six weeks old, and they're the loves of my life. My best work.' The couple were often spotted taking the dogs for a stroll in the park.

As a newcomer to the world of celebrity, Sienna initially had trouble keeping her feelings to herself. She wanted to shout from the rooftops about her love for Jude and the tabloid press were more than willing to listen. Very early on, though, Jude taught her to be guarded. His previous relationship had been a victim of overzealous press intrusion and he wouldn't allow it to happen again. 'I have a tendency to be incapable of concealing any sort of feeling, which has got me into trouble. I speak my mind and then it [is printed] all wrong,' confessed Sienna.

Suddenly, Sienna Miller had a profile. Every morning, she woke up to find photographers camped on her doorstep and even a trip to the local shop proved to be an undercover operation. For a girl who prized her 'ordinary' lifestyle, this new level of media scrutiny would take some getting used to. Defiantly, she refused to buckle under the pressures and expectations of fame. 'You can't whinge about it because, you know what, you make your bed and then you have to sleep in it,' she said stoically. 'In a dream world I'd like to do what I do and not get photographed with my dogs, picking up shit every day, but, if that goes with the territory, I would rather have that than not do this.'

But she did find this new level of media scrutiny difficult to comprehend. Surely the public weren't really bothered about her every move and murmur? Like Sienna, they surely had something better to do? 'I struggle with it,' Sienna said of her 24-hour tabloid surveillance. 'I'd be lying if I said I didn't. It's a level of invasion that happened so quickly and not because of work or anything that I felt had justified some sort of interest.' Instead, the paparazzi were more keen to photograph Sienna if 'I'm wearing a nice bag or I'm walking my dogs with my boyfriend'.

The actress lamented that in today's gossip-obsessed society Hollywood stars had been demystified. 'What happened to the glamour?' she asked. 'There's something so gorgeous about old Hollywood, these people always looking fantastic. And now you get paparazzi photos of people with a burger half in their mouth or their finger up their nose or pulling their knickers out of their bum…'

While she'd learned to adapt to her new circumstances, Sienna steadfastly maintained that nothing else in her life had altered. 'My life hasn't changed, I haven't changed and my friends haven't changed… I'm not inherently self-conscious but, if people start to scrutinise you, you kind of battle with things which before and in my nature I'd never ever have given a flying hoot to. If you have a hangover, wearing pyjamas and you want to get a pint of milk, there's a slight element of – what will they say?' Defiantly, Sienna refused to pander to such insecurities. 'There's also a rebellion that comes with it, which is fuck it, I don't give a shit. And, thank God, I'm still on that side.'

Sienna soon became accustomed to photographers lurking at every street corner. But, while she had reached a level of acceptance with the situation, Jude was infuriated by their persistence. Partly this was because he felt a need to protect his younger and less experienced girlfriend. She had an innocence he admired and didn't want to see destroyed. One particular incident illustrated the point clearly. Jude and Sienna had been drinking in Primrose Hill, when they decided to take a cab west and go out to a restaurant. A photographer had been trailing the pair and stepped out to ask Jude for a photograph. Jude lost his temper and started throwing not only expletives, but also coins at the stunned man. Sienna bundled her boyfriend into a restaurant doorway, in a bid to stop him emptying his pockets. The pair then jumped in another cab and zoomed off into the night.

'You have to accept it and you have to be gracious about it,' shrugged Sienna, in explanation of her apathy towards the press. 'Of course, I would certainly rather it wasn't there – be it good or bad. And I know I could have had it a lot worse than I have had it.'

Jude, however, had far less patience with the media. The two had never enjoyed an easy relationship. Over time he'd come to resent their constant prying and interference in his life. Jude was a fiercely private creature and yet most of his private life had been lived out in the public domain. When reporters at the Orange British Academy Film Awards quizzed Jude about his relationship with Sienna, he was furious. One fearless journalist asked how the besotted couple had spent their first Valentine's Day. Jude simply turned on his heel and walked away. Inside, he was a ball of anger, but he wasn't about to indulge the tabloids in another story. He would simply refuse to talk about his personal life. It was as simple as that.

But one thing that did irritate Sienna was outright lies. That she couldn't abide. 'Complete and utter fabrications that I've never said or would ever dream of saying or would ever happen to me!' she fumed. 'There's this weird thing that keeps coming back where, apparently, I met Kevin Spacey in a bar and said, "I can't believe I'm sitting in a bar drinking champagne with Kevin Bacon!" And he said,

"Spacey." And I said, "Isn't it?" I've never met Kevin Spacey and, had I, I think I would know the difference between him and Kevin Bacon. It's like, who – bored at their desk – is making up stuff like this? Then there's this other quote, apparently of mine, that goes, "I still pinch myself when I wake up with Jude because he's such a gorgeous man." When I wake up with Jude what I do is my own business, but, believe me, I don't pinch myself! It's degrading! You have to sit there and kind of stomach it and think, Oh, well, no one's reading it, but it keeps coming back.'

Tabloid stories also put a strain on her relationship with Jude. Only recently, she'd been forced to look at pictures of Jude kissing Natalie Portman on the set of *Closer* and read a story suggesting he'd fallen in love with somebody else. In another article, a body-language expert had been invited to pass his judgement on photos of the couple together. He concluded Sienna was clingy and needy while Jude was fed up and disinterested. 'I know that I've made my bed and I have to lie in it,' said Sienna of the inevitable press interest that accompanies any high-profile relationship. 'What I don't understand, though, is why people have to be so negative. Being so analysed and judged is just terrible. Why can't something ever say that we are very happy and very in love and celebrate it?'

The couple preferred not to waste their valuable time discussing ridiculous stories in the press. They'd never calculated the degree to which their relationship would be put under public scrutiny. 'You have to accept a certain degree of publicity, but the amount we are scrutinised as a couple is unhealthy,' Sienna complained. 'But it's just not the kind of thing you sit down and have a conversation about, is it? "Right, if we get together, this is how your life is gonna change." People are very cynical about the fact two actors get together on a film set, but how are you supposed to meet people? Yes, I'd have been stupid if I hadn't been conscious that there would be an interest in it. But urgh!!!'

Being famous had never been key to Sienna's career agenda and now she was beginning to actively underplay her newfound status. What particularly irritated her was the suggestion that she'd only hooked up with Jude to raise her own profile. But Sienna was no attention-seeker. 'I don't think anyone, unless they're stupid, would say they wanted to be famous. In some ways, I was naive because I looked at people like Kate Winslet and certain British actors who manage to juggle a home life that they kept very private and a career doing films and theatre and I thought that I could do the same thing. Fame wasn't something that I was drawn to or wanted or looked for – I never actually planned to do films. I always wanted to do theatre but when it's a great part and a lot of money... But I think next year I'd like to do a play. Only because the thought of it petrifies me.'

Fame for the wrong reasons was a concern that gradually began to grate on Sienna; she was desperate to be more than some Hollywood hunk's arm candy. 'I'm not very happy about it to be honest,' she complained. 'It makes me uncomfortable because I don't think it's as a result of having a film come out, I think it's as a result of being scrutinised because of the relationship I'm in. If it was because of work, I think I'd feel more justified and more comfortable with it.'

Matthew Vaughn, director of Sienna's first film, *Layer Cake*, echoed those sentiments: 'Hopefully Sienna won't fall into the trap of being a celebrity more than an actress in people's eyes,' he commented.

While some cynics might argue Sienna's relationship with Jude had helped boost her career, in actual fact it had been something of a hindrance. 'The second film I did was *Alfie* and I met Jude and fell in love with a man who happened to be a very successful, very talented actor. And all the attention I received was only because I happened to fall in love with someone who was famous. It happened in reverse to the way I would have liked it to or planned it,' she sighed. Sienna Miller would have preferred to have had a career before the fame.

Sienna feared her celebrity status would distract from her ultimate goal. If an audience already had a preconceived identity of her, it would be difficult for them to accept her as any other character. 'I think anonymity as an actor is the most important thing,' she claimed. 'It's very hard to convince people you're a character if they know who you really are… And also people are sick of you. They don't want to go and watch you when they can pick up a magazine every day and there you are, wearing a nice pair of jeans or a pretty coat or having a fight with your boyfriend.

One perfect example of Sienna's dilemma was her invitation to appear in *Vanity Fair* as part of their Hollywood March '05 issue. Sienna was ecstatic when her agent called up with the news, clapping her hands wildly and letting out a gasp. Although she'd appeared in fashion magazines as a faceless model, being selected as part of a Hollywood line-up surely cemented her identity as an actress. Jude agreed that it would be a good idea for his eager girlfriend to do the shoot.

It would take place at a photo studio in LA and a chauffeur-driven limousine arrived to collect Sienna from her hotel. Breathing deeply, Sienna tried not to look nervous. She was taken to her palatial dressing room. Champagne and bowls of fresh fruit filled the room. She'd certainly never been treated this well in her modelling days.

'Sienna, darling,' her appointed stylist called over, pointing to a clothes rail. 'Could you come and try these?' Together they picked out a head-turning outfit; a Karl Lagerfeld jacket and Gina Bacconi skirt. Sienna tentatively walked over to take her place in the stellar line-up of Tinseltown's glittering stars. Present that day were Uma Thurman, Kate Winslet, Cate Blanchett and Scarlett Johansson. Between them, the group shared 16 Oscar and Bafta nominations. Without the A-list credentials to match, Sienna did look a little like a fish out of water. With only two films to her names (*Alfie* having been a disappointing box-office flop), she hardly merited inclusion on the grounds of achievement. Sienna was uncomfortably aware of that fact.

The magazine, however, insisted they had chosen the actress on her merit. 'She is going to be the next big thing,' enthused Krista Smith, the magazine's West Coast editor who had made the selection. Unfortunately, she only went on to confirm suspicions that this wasn't the sole reason for choosing Sienna for the shoot, by adding, 'Plus she has a fantastic boyfriend.'

Whereas, by her own admission, Sienna had launched her career in the token role of 'the girl', now she'd been earmarked as 'the girlfriend'. It was a tag she'd have difficulty trying to shake. Even in front of other celebrities, she was introduced as 'Jude's girlfriend'. Her inclusion in the hallowed Hollywood circle was alarmingly provisional.

Jude was conscious of Sienna's anxieties and agreed it would be better if they both distanced themselves professionally. The couple had originally looked at several scripts together, but Jude quickly decided it was a bad idea. He was also frightened that the disastrous box-office results of his Natural Nylon film *Sky Captain and the World of Tomorrow* might reflect badly on anyone who chose to work with him in the future.

Claims that Jude had become Sienna's mentor also niggled the now fiercely independent actress. 'Jude is not my mentor,' she snapped abruptly, although she conceded,

'Having a boyfriend who has experienced it all before is helpful.' During interviews, when the topic of Jude came up in conversation, Sienna would quickly clam her mouth shut. 'No, no, no. I don't, I can't, I don't want to talk about it. My relationship is something I want to keep as private as possible because, to be really honest, it's about as non-private as it could be! That little bit that is mine I want to keep mine. Ours.'

Sienna was under a ridiculous amount of pressure to deliver the goods. While other young actors had the luxury of developing their talents behind closed doors, she felt uncomfortably exposed. Every mistake she made would be noted by critics and held against her for ever more. 'I certainly felt more of a pressure to be all right as an actress,' she lamented. 'It's not like I'm in a place where I feel safe and set about my future. It's still very much up in the air.'

Taunts about her acting ability upset the sensitive actress and she felt the need to prove people wrong. Critics had dismissed her as tabloid fodder and nothing more than a pretty clothes horse. Sienna was desperate to be taken seriously as an actress. She loved her craft and would hate it to be overshadowed by her celebrity status. 'I take my job very seriously. It kills me and I love it,' she said passionately. 'I find it quite alarming because I'm so desperate to be taken seriously as an actress and not be just thought of as Jude Law's girlfriend who is sometimes on the cover of a newspaper for no reason other than having worn a short skirt at Glastonbury.' But, remaining upbeat about her future, the young star knew she was improving. 'I do feel as if I'm going through a massive growing-up process where I know what I want to be and what I can be, but getting there takes a lot of inner strength.' If mistakes were to be made along the way, then so be it. Sienna would only use these to her advantage. 'When I mess up, I try and learn from that so I don't regret anything. I try to make everything a learning curve.'

Now settled in her relationship, Sienna was ready to make headway with her career. It was time to free herself from the shackles of being 'Jude Law's girlfriend' or the lowly pawn in the 'Jude/Sadie love scandal'. It was time to stand on her own two feet as Sienna Miller the actress. She was hungry for a creative challenge. Fortunately, the boost she needed was lying just around the corner.

EIGHT

Enter Casanova

IF asked to drum up a list of dream roles, Sienna could roll off countless choices. Thanks to an interest in history and literature, she'd always dreamed of playing in a period drama. And, as the archetypal English rose, her good looks were more than fitting for the part. 'One day I'd like to play Medea – when I'm a bit more tortured,' she mused. 'It's heavy but as an actress it's pretty fantastic. I've always liked to play Anne Boleyn; for some reason I always loved her.'

In all honesty, Sienna was open to any suggestion at that stage in her career. What she was very clear about were the parts she didn't want to play. 'I want to do everything apart from being just "the girl" or "the love interest".' Instead, she described her ideal roles as 'meaty, intelligent or strong or illuminated women'.

In mid-2004, acclaimed Swedish director Lasse Hallström (*Chocolat, Cider House Rules, The Shipping News*) was casting for his new movie *Casanova*, a £40-million retelling of the infamous Italian seducer's tale. *Brokeback Mountain* star Heath Ledger had already signed up as the male lead. Now Lasse was after someone suitable to play the female lead of Francesca, the defiant intellect who refuses to fall under Casanova's spell, and who subsequently becomes the apple of his eye. Lasse put out feelers in both LA and London. When Sienna's agent Dallas read the script, he knew it would be the perfect part for his client.

Sienna was instantly hooked. For a start, the idea of a period drama really appealed: 'I was getting into a little bit of a niche where I was perceived as very modern, because I think I am quite modern, and I just wanted to be able to show that I could do something different where I wasn't blonde and I kept my clothes on,' she said, with a laugh.

Secondly, she had always been a fan of Lasse's and the opportunity to work with him seemed too great to let drift by. 'Lasse is one of my heroes and he made one of the best films I've ever seen – *My Life as a Dog*,' she bubbled with audible enthusiasm. 'It's one of my top five films of all time. And you can tell by his films that he is a great guy.'

Finally, and most importantly, Sienna was attracted to both the script and the character of Francesca. 'It's a brilliant script!' she told Dallas. 'I think that era in Venice was so decadent and debauched, the wonderful clothes and the legend of this romantic Lothario was just very appealing.' She was also relieved to have been offered the opportunity to try for a part far removed from the usual roles she was given. 'For a woman my age, you don't very often see a part that is that meaty.' Since playing Tammy in *Layer Cake*, countless scripts for roles in a similar vein had been passed her way. But she was fed up with being 'the girl'. There was so much more to her talents. It was time to flex and stretch her acting abilities. Francesca seemed the ideal part for exactly that. 'She is an early feminist, dresses up as a man, she's outspoken, strong, fierce, feisty and sword-fighting,' squealed Sienna, listing the character's most appealing qualities. 'It's a dream role.'

In the film, Francesca is an intelligent woman, desperate to be educated and go to university. Unlike other women happy to take their place 'in the hearth and in the bed', she is determined to follow her own will. But living in a repressed society, where women have few rights, she is forced to dress as a man in order to gain access to the university. Having developed a deep understanding of the part, Sienna felt she could do it justice. She even drew comparisons between herself and Francesca. 'I think when you play a character you have to be able to relate to certain aspects!' she said, before adding, 'But I think I'm more stubborn than she is and not nearly as intelligent. I aspire to be more like her because she is so outspoken and unattached to what people think. She's a great woman, but I'm not as bold and a bit more vulnerable.'

Sienna attended a preliminary audition and then screen-tested alongside Heath Ledger in LA. She then waited anxiously as the studio decided whether or not they needed to cast a well-known name. Several had been in the running, although Sienna preferred 'not to get involved in that side'. But, just as she had done with *Alfie*, Sienna did a lot of begging for the part. 'I really, really wanted it,' she impressed. Her persistence paid off – the part was hers.

In truth, Lasse had known from the start that he wanted to cast Sienna. 'She stood out from the start,' he claimed. 'There's something about the Brits. If you compare the American girls to the British ones, [there's] a certain elegance, a certain class that, if you're lucky, comes with English actors. And she's a classy actress with great instinct. Francesca is an early feminist and I wanted someone with a strong personality and intelligence to play her. She also has the kind of charisma and charm that makes you believe in a character. I think she is a natural talent.'

Only once filming had commenced would Sienna realise why her casting process had taken so long. 'I think the reason was that he just wants to make sure you are perfect for the part so when it comes to shooting it's like, "Right it's yours, you can't do any wrong, you are this person."'

At the time of Sienna's initial audition, *Alfie* was still in post-production. Lasse went to the editing room and watched a couple of scenes from *Alfie*. He also did some homework by quizzing Charles about Sienna's performance on set. 'They tend to research and find out if you are nightmare and refuse to get up in the mornings,' joked Sienna, before adding, 'And, no, I'm not a nightmare. I'm just horrible in the mornings.'

As soon as Sienna heard the part was hers, she diligently set to work on researching the role. 'For certain things I tend to be quite spontaneous, and I'm a crammer. I just don't work well as somebody who sits there doing work for months and months because I have quite a short attention span. But I did for *Casanova*.' First of all, Sienna tried to imagine what it must feel like to live in a society where women are repressed. Fortunately for her, it was something she'd never experienced before. 'I read a lot about Emily Pankhurst and the suffragists. I looked at societies where women feel very repressed – like in Baghdad.' She was also keen to capture the mood of 18th-century Venice. 'I read a book called *The Venetian Love Story*, which is set around the same period that we were concentrating on. I had Casanova's memoirs and I dabbled in Venetian history.' Finally, she attempted to hone her acting craft by watching actors who had taken on similar roles. 'I watched Judi Dench in *Mrs Brown* a lot, just women who are strong. There was a lot to be done.'

Sienna was especially pleased to be playing such a formidable character, as it gave her the opportunity to be a role model for other young women. 'She sticks to her morals, she's intelligent and she's not afraid to be different.

I think it's very hard in the society we live in for young girls not to conform, especially when there are so many generic comedies out there where blonde girls in tank tops are flicking their hair. Here's this rather intelligent, debating woman. I think she's a good role model. For me as well, you know.'

But the role of Francesca was not only intellectually demanding. A number of physical preparations were also required for the part. Sienna agreed to pile on a few pounds for the part and even wore a brown wig. She looked a million miles away from blonde bombshell Nikki in *Alfie*. 'It wasn't about being glamorous. She's not supposed to be particularly attractive,' explained Sienna, before modestly correcting herself, 'Not that I am!'

'I wanted to look very different from how I look normally. She [Francesca] wasn't out there to try to get a man, so I didn't want anything about her to be ostentatious.' Sienna's make-up artist suggested they use powder to make her look pale, although Sienna would later confess that she'd been desperate to wear a bit of blusher. They also added eyebrows and changed her hairline. 'It's not a pretty wig,' said Sienna, screwing up her nose. Finally, she agreed to put on the weight for the part, although she would later confess, 'I told everyone I put on weight for the part, but really it's because I'd been in Venice chugging down pasta and tiramisu.'

As usual, Sienna quickly acquainted herself with the wardrobe team and was heavily involved in her character's costume. She loved rummaging through piles of period clothing and on the eve of filming had been excited about wearing a corset.

'I can't wait!' she told friends. 'It will be so much fun and imagine what it will do for my cleavage!'

'You wait,' they warned her. 'Within a few hours you'll be in agony.'

Of course, they were right. At first, Sienna found the rib-cracking garment useful for getting into character. 'The costume is gorgeous and gives you so much idea of the character when you put these clothes on. It makes you feel very repressed, which my character was struggling with in the repression of that society. You can hardly breathe and your organs are squashed within an inch of their lives! We did it very authentically.' She described the experience as being 'like Vivien Leigh in *Gone With The Wind*. You have to hold on to a pole to get strapped in.' And there were several other benefits: 'I didn't realise I had breasts until I made *Casanova*. I loved my cleavage. I sat there pressing it for ages. Also, they painted a little mole on my breast, which I adored.'

But, as predicted, within half an hour, the novelty had worn off and Sienna couldn't wait to get rid of the thing. 'It squeezes your skin and it really hurts,' she complained. 'I was totally strapped into this thing. Your waist is squeezed down and your boobs are squeezed up.' Sienna also found it difficult to eat in costume. 'I like to eat a lot and tried to squeeze down sandwiches, which would get stuck.' It wasn't quite the glamorous look the actress had imagined. Unable to lie down because of their 'big bum bustles', Sienna and her co-star Lena Olin were forced to perch uncomfortably. Added to the fact they couldn't mess up their wigs, the women had to assume some rather strange positions. 'Boy, did we laugh!' recalls Sienna. For the entire four and a half months of shooting, Heath Ledger even referred to his co-star endearingly as 'big-bum'. Shooting in the blazing summer heat also proved to be unbearable. 'We shot everything in palazzos that had no air conditioning, so it was like 110 degrees.' In the end, Sienna was so fed up with the garment she tried to burn it! 'I was caught trying to steal it in the middle of the night to torch it,' she jokes. But discomfort wasn't the only inconvenience Sienna's costumes were causing. 'Plus, I couldn't have a fag because it would mess up my big curly pube wig.'

As it turned out, filming *Casanova* would expose Sienna to a whole host of new experiences. In one scene, her character was required to take part in a sword fight. It was a skill Sienna had to learn on the job. 'I'm not the most co-ordinated person, so it took a bit of work, but it was really great. It's lovely learning something new!' In another scene, the script demanded she dress up as a 12-year-old boy! Sienna spent hours at home trying to drop her voice an octave. She felt quite ridiculous in front of the camera and wondered what people would think of her. 'What have I done? Everyone is going to laugh!' she cringed. 'But this is a dream job,' she admitted. 'I've ridden horses, I've dressed up as a boy. It's pretty extraordinary and diverse.'

Admittedly, Sienna was daunted by the prospect of playing such a challenging role with such a revered cast, but after only a few days on set her fears were quickly laid to rest: 'Lasse's great gift is creating a set that is so harmonious and so easy and any intimidation just evaporated.' She went on to praise her director further: 'He is just very generous and very calm and very focused and knows exactly what he wants. So it's been a great experience. I would have jumped off a cliff to work with Lasse. I've watched pretty much all of his films and working with him cements pretty much what I thought before – the man's a genius.'

Returning the compliment, Lasse enthused, 'She's a film star, make no mistake. And a pleasure to work with. It's rare to encounter such confidence in a young actor.'

As a director, Lasse's preferred method of working was to hand most of the creative responsibility over to his actors. 'It's really interesting,' explained Sienna. 'He has a very subtle way of working. It's not that he comes on and directs every line. What he does is cleverly hand the responsibility over to you, so you're kind of playing against yourself. You're doing it for you, not for anyone else. And he sits back and gives very subtle kinds of guides, but is not full on. Working with him, I've no idea what he is doing, which I love. You watch him and he is so calm and centred and still and you know there is so much going on in there. He directs us, obviously, and he has a very clear idea. As far as I'm concerned and I haven't spoken to him about this, he has this entire film cut, finished, credits, everything in his head. He's seen it. So he is shooting only what he is going to cut, which is extraordinary and you just kind of sit back and watch this man who you trust implicitly. And I think he trusts you. There's this dynamic of respect.' Being a young actress in her first lead role, Sienna was quite overwhelmed by the experience. Lasse was patient and understanding. 'He's like, "Just keep doing what you're doing. You're doing great!" Little words of encouragement or nudges here and there, so you don't feel like you're doing it wrong.' According to Sienna, the overall effect was 'an energy on set that's calm and conducive to creativity'.

Sienna described *Casanova* as 'a farcical romp set in this lovely era. It's flamboyant, decadent and sumptuous.' Tom Stoppard, responsible for the Gwyneth Paltrow and Joseph Fiennes box-office smash *Shakespeare in Love*, even had a hand in writing the screenplay. According to Sienna, however, *Casanova* was a 'lot more slapstick'. Although she was required to play little comedy herself, performing with other actors did give her a good understanding of the medium. In particular, she commended her co-star Oliver Platt for his ability to play both a comically entertaining and emotionally engaging character. 'Oliver has done an extraordinary job with that character, who, on paper, was just one big fat joke. He somehow managed to make this part convincing. I don't know how he's done it. He comes on with his fat suit and you care about him... He's just very convincing, on top of being hilarious, and you really care about that character. I think he kind of runs away with the film.'

In contrast, Sienna's own character was quite serious. 'She is the serious one in the script, because she is going through these real inner dilemmas about being a woman.' At times, she found it hard not to slip into a slapstick pantomime role. 'Lasse was very good at reminding me just how depressed a character she is! I was desperate at times to do a wink and a nudge and a little pout or a flick of the fan and I had to stay on this rather miserable journey, and it was tough. It was probably the biggest challenge, along with the corset.'

But, while Sienna was obliged to be serious on screen, there was plenty of opportunity for frivolity once the cameras had stopped rolling. In between takes, she and the cast would constantly crack jokes. Filming on location in Venice made the whole experience surreal in itself. The city was prone to monthly bouts of flooding, known as *aqua alta* (high water), and Sienna recalls how on one occasion the entire cast were trapped knee deep in water. 'We were battling against flooding one day, up to our thighs in water and crying with laughter.'

Sienna recalled how Oliver Platt would entertain the cast by singing ridiculous songs while dressed in his fat suit. Sienna and several other crew members were travelling in a water taxi between locations. In a jovial mood, Oliver started to hum the melody of 'Skip to my Lou'. Very soon, he adapted his own lyrics: 'Trapped in my fat suit one fine day, do-dah, do-dah. Had too many coffees, oh do-dah day' – at which point he let out the sound of an enormous fart. Everyone erupted into laughter, before joining in his silly song. 'We'd all be on these boats, singing along,' says Sienna, smiling fondly at the memory.

'We did not stop laughing for five months. I know it sounds a cliché, but we were about as close as you could possibly be, and I think it really comes across in the film that we're having a really good time.' On another occasion, Heath had Sienna rolling around on the floor when he split his trousers doing a lunge during the sword-fighting scene.

The two young actors quickly became the film's onset jokers. 'He is completely stupid on set, which I love,' said Sienna of her co-star. 'He is the most fantastically laid-back person to work with.' Perhaps their funniest moment was shared while filming the food-fight scenes. 'Cut!' called Lasse, satisfied he had enough material. The set was a mess. Overturned platters of meat littered the floor, while red wine seeped from broken glass goblets. Noticing a pile of grapes on the table had escaped unscathed, Sienna tossed one into her mouth.

'Go on then,' taunted Heath. 'How many of those can you fit in your big mouth?'

In a playful mood, Sienna rose to the challenge. 'We'll see, shall we!' she said, stuffing two giant fistfuls of fruit in her mouth. Juice dribbled from her bottom lip; it was certainly a sight to behold. Trying desperately hard not to giggle, with Heath sniggering in the background, she walked over to the DP and mumbled, 'Can we shoot around this?' Needless to say, the whole place erupted into hysterics.

'I just turned into a child when I was on set,' shrugged Sienna in explanation. 'We were quite naughty.' But she proudly adds, 'I managed eight and a half grapes in my mouth. That's the record.'

Very early on, Sienna and Heath became great friends and Sienna even referred to their relationship as being 'like brother and sister'. She believes the foundations of a good friendship made the sexual chemistry on screen even more convincing. 'I don't think there's any formula,' she maintained. 'You either have it with people or you don't. With Heath and I, we're quite similar as people, but not too serious. So there was a great rapport from day one. We became very good friends and I trusted him as an actor. Even from that, you can get along so well with someone and have absolutely zero chemistry. But eventually it naturally evolved. We were both on the same page about what we wanted the relationship to be.'

In terms of Francesca's romantic motivation, Sienna found it easy to sympathise with her character. Although keen to find love, she only falls for Casanova once he sacrifices himself for her. 'I am hopelessly romantic as a person – but I'm a girl, I think,' she confessed. 'Hopelessly and hopefully romantic.'

But when it came to filming the kissing scene Sienna still had her apprehensions. After all, Heath had only recently appeared in the Oscar-nominated gay romance, *Brokeback Mountain*. 'He told me about kissing Jake, so if he thinks that was better I'm in trouble!' she joked to Jude.

Eventually, the pair became so close they were even happy to walk around semi-naked in front of each other. 'We were in these rooms with a curtain separating us – as opposed to using our own trailers. The boys were farting next door and we were chucking food over each other. It was like being back at school – it was such a laugh. We all saw each other's bits and bobs several times.'

Prior to working with Heath, Sienna had seen a few of his films. 'He was really brilliant in *Monster's Ball*,' she recalls. 'It was a really small role but when I watched it I remember thinking that he was so captivating and interesting.' But, preferring to research her co-star in person, Sienna didn't go out of her way to hire any of his DVDs. 'To be honest, I hadn't seen a lot of what he had done before but as soon as I met him I liked him and I knew he was perfect for the role. I think a lot of actors would have walked in playing the greatest lover of all time and puff their chests out and pout and feel very self-important. And Heath being the way that he is, and the actor that he is, sat back and allowed it very much to be an ensemble piece. He didn't over-pose or over-pout. He did it as a real character. It was my first big role and he was fantastic to me.' Illustrating her newfound respect for the actor, she continued, 'As an actor I think he is really brave. He has a lot of work about to come out that will really show his range.'

Filming *Casanova* gave Sienna the much-needed confidence boost she'd been after. And it showed. On set, she was a vibrant ball of energy able to keep the cast constantly entertained. She blazed like sunshine and few could resist the temptation to bask in her warmth of character. In conversation, she made people feel as if they were the only living being in the universe. 'She's a lot of fun on set,' revealed her co-star Oliver Platt. 'A dice-playing, joke-telling vixen.'

Sienna Miller was in her element. 'Certainly I feel more confident,' she admitted. 'Just doing a project like this that I'm really proud to be involved in.' Finally, she hoped the public focus would no longer be on her relationship, what she was wearing or, given her past celluloid experience, what she was *not* wearing. 'In this film I keep my corset firmly tight!' she grinned. At last Sienna would be laid bare figuratively rather than literally. Finally, critics could judge her on her acting skills alone. 'This is nothing to do with me being sexy. There is nothing for me to hide behind,' she proudly boasted. 'I'm looking forward to being seen as something other than a young naked wannabe actor.'

Oliver Platt added, 'I'm very excited for her because, when people see the movie, it will take the focus off her off-screen activities. It was incredible how still and mature her performance was. She has the innate knowledge of letting the camera come to her.'

No wonder the beautiful actress was walking round with an indelible smile etched on her face. She had the man and now it looked as if she had the career to match. Every piece of the jigsaw was fitting perfectly into place.

NINE

A Venetian Love Affair

IT was difficult for Sienna not to fall in love with Venice, that much-revered city of romance. And an escape from London couldn't have come at a better time for her. As soon as she set foot in the Italian city, she felt as if she'd walked into another time period and another world. Sienna lived in Vienna for five months. She'd never been before, but after a period of time she felt 'practically Venetian'. She recalls her period of stay as blissful. Even though she was only a two-hour plane journey from London, she felt completely removed from the rest of the world. 'Venice is like a Disneyland for adults!' she told friends. During the summer, hordes of tourists would jam-pack the narrow streets. But, as the winter months drew in, so the crowds grew smaller. During that period, the city was at its most beautiful.

Sienna had rented a small apartment behind the fish market. Every day she would step out and wave good morning to the owners. Outside her bedroom window on the street below was a fruit stall filled with a colourful assortment of exotic items. Sienna loved to watch the local people go about their daily business. Theirs seemed a simple life and one that instantly appealed to an uncomplicated girl whose life had been far too complex thus far.

Determined to feel at home, Sienna put a great deal of effort into making the apartment her own. Beautiful silk throws draped the furnishings, while numerous black-and-white photographs filled the wall space. There were pictures of Sienna with her friends, photos of her mum and, of course, portraits of Jude. Her eye regularly fell on one particular picture, taken in New York. Hollywood film star or not, there was no denying Jude was a handsome man. She missed him like crazy, but at least the photographs could keep her company.

After only a few weeks, her wardrobes were full to the brim with haute-couture clothes. Once designers caught a whiff of the fact that the latest fashion muse was in town, they couldn't wait to adorn her with all the latest cuts. From Missoni to Fendi, labels were falling over themselves to give Sienna whatever she wanted from their latest collections. Every day, a new fashion PR would drop by her apartment with a range of goods in an assortment of colours. All Sienna had to do was take her pick. 'I do feel spoiled!' she confessed to friends.

During the week, Sienna had an early start. It took almost four hours to fix her corset and wig. Every morning, a boat would arrive to pick her up. 'There's no car waiting for you!' she complained – in jest – to her mum. Thankfully, it wasn't a gondola! Those were strictly for the tourists. A novelty at first, Sienna had grown sick of hearing Frank Sinatra's 'My Way' bleated by gondoliers as they passed beneath her bedroom window, leaving a flurry of rose petals in their wake.

Trundling along the Grand Canal and watching the sunrise would become one of Sienna's lasting memories of Venice. The light was indescribable, a light peachy smudge with a slightly syrupy orange hue. 'It was ridiculous. It was a dream,' she later recalled. On occasion, the boat would stop off to collect Heath. But she could count the number of times that happened on one hand. 'Nothing got Heath out of bed before he absolutely had to!' she later recalled, with a laugh.

Admittedly, Venice wasn't the most practical place in which to shoot a feature film. 'Initially we were struggling with having camera equipment on boats,' Sienna explained. The light in Venice was also famously capricious, making the city look like a completely different place simply within a matter of 24 hours. 'We could never really predict what was going to happen.' Of course, the crew could have chosen to film *Casanova* elsewhere. It probably would have made life easier! But Lasse was adamant. 'He wouldn't do it unless it was entirely shot here. They have a Venetian set in Luxembourg so we could have easily ended up there and thank Christ we didn't. You could also have done a lot of studio stuff, but you just get so much, an essence, a wonderful vibe from actually being here. And such a sense of a place. I think it's impossible to re-create the light anywhere else.'

Sienna was thrilled the crew had chosen to abide by Lasse's wishes. 'It's so fantastic to be shooting in a place where a film is set. If ever you needed something to get you into a role, this would be it!' she told Jude enthusiastically. Even to this day, Sienna still counts the magical city as one of her favourite places: 'It was possibly the most heavenly place that you could make a film in the world.'

Friends had warned Sienna that Venice might be more of a sensory experience than she'd bargained for. Principally, they were referring to the city's canals, which notoriously kicked up a stink during the hotter months. Sienna wasn't deterred. 'Everybody said it's going to be really smelly, and I didn't find that at all,' she said, before adding, 'I probably lost my sense of smell a few years ago living in a big city!' But as far as Sienna was concerned nothing could shatter her fairytale illusion. 'It wasn't smelly; it was gorgeous.'

One mistake Sienna did make was to watch Nicolas Roeg's Venice-set shocker *Don't Look Now* prior to her trip. The cult 1970s movie tells the story of a couple who move to Venice after their young daughter drowns. A psychic claims to see the spirit of the young child, who appears to be walking the streets in a red cloak. 'The stupidest thing I've ever done,' she shudders. Although Venice was relatively small in size, the city was a labyrinth of narrow, meandering streets. On the way home to her flat, Sienna would quite often confuse her bearings and find herself lost. It was on those occasions, while walking along an empty backstreet, that she'd recall the film and start running very fast.

Aside from the horror stories, Sienna loved the Italian lifestyle. She was particularly impressed by the food and drink on offer and would regularly order a bottle of rosé with lunch. As for food, she could quite happily devour plates of pasta all day long (she was currently on two plates a day). 'It's lovely,' she says, salivating at the thought. And dessert wasn't a problem either. 'I'm averaging three ice creams a day here, which is not good, but they're too good not to have one. I like the ones with nuts.' The cast would often go out together for big dinners and sample the local dishes on offer. Sienna revelled in the opportunity to develop strong and lasting friendships. 'We've had a lot of big cast dinners. I know it's a cliché and you have to say it, but we are really, really close as a group, as a cast. We'd go out for dinners and drink wine and find these restaurants where they have pianos in the corner and sit and sing around the piano. It's perfect.' Unfortunately, Sienna failed to pick up much of the Italian language during her stay.

She blamed the fact that she'd learned Spanish in the past, which she felt 'hindered my Italian. It's not good.' In fact, all she could communicate was: 'A glass of white wine, please' along with various other items from the menu. On her days off, Sienna would visit galleries or go to the beach and play volleyball. 'There's so much to do, so much inspiration!' she enthused.

Sienna was even lucky enough to be in Venice during the famous annual film festival. The experience was incredible. As she sat in the foyer of the Hotel Cipriani sipping on a cocktail, she watched all manner of film stars drift past. In just 12 months' time, she would be the one fielding reporters and attending premieres for her own film, *Casanova*. For now, she was comfortable soaking up the atmosphere.

One day, she noticed Al Pacino sitting at the next table. 'I have such a crush on him!' she confessed to a friend who is sat with her. 'I actually don't know what to do! As luck would have it, her co-star Charlie Cox had wandered over to chat with the famous star, in town to promote his film *The Merchant of Venice*. He summoned Sienna over.

'Hi, I'm Sienna,' she said, nervously extending her hand and almost snagging her delicate Missoni dress in the process.

'Pleased to meet you, Diana!' Pacino growled in reply.

'No, I'm Si-e-n-n-a,' she enunciated, somewhat embarrassed. Fortunately, she could see the funny side. Compared to the Hollywood legends around her, she was small fry. Her feet still firmly locked on planet Earth, she was able to appreciate that.

During Sienna's stint in Venice, Jude came to visit her on several occasions. Out of long-lens shot, the pair enjoyed the privacy of travelling about town by boat. On one of the first occasions Jude came to visit, Sienna took him out to an excellent restaurant she'd discovered only days before. Having come straight from the set, she was still dressed in full costume complete with wig and corset. People stopped, stared and shot her strange glances, but she didn't seem to care. As far as she was concerned, the food was great and that was all that mattered. 'I love this restaurant,' she cooed to Jude, who agreed the chef had done a fine job.

Jude returned to the set with Sienna to meet some of her co-stars. As the couple walked towards Sienna's makeshift trailer, she noticed several bright flashes.

'What was that?' she asked Jude, slightly stunned.

'Oh, probably just tourists,' he muttered.

The couple thought nothing more of it.

A few days later, Sienna's PR assistant arrived in the city to co-ordinate several press interviews. She arrived at Sienna's flat with several tabloid newspapers tucked under her arm. As Sienna leafed through the pages over breakfast, she was shocked to discover several photographs of her and Jude on set. 'How on earth did they get those?' she enquired. Amusingly, they'd managed to capture Sienna just as she was having her wig adjusted. All she had on her head was the flesh-coloured skull cap that keeps the wig in place. The journalists had a field day and mockingly suggested Jude had been caught kissing a small, bald boy. Sienna had to admit the picture was quite funny. She picked up the high-spec Motorola mobile she'd recently acquired from Jude after telling him 'it looked naff'. Struggling hard to get the words out between fits of giggles, she told him the news.

Thankfully, though, now the tabloids had their comedy shot, they decided to leave Sienna alone. Besides, using long-lens cameras on the speedy Vaporetto boats did prove quite tricky. Whenever Jude came out to visit, the couple revelled in their relative freedom. Now on first-name terms with most of the locals, Sienna felt quite comfortable wandering round the crumbling city. It seemed that, at every trattoria she passed, somebody would step outside and greet her with a hug and kiss, insisting she absolutely must come inside for a glass of Prosecco. But, in spite of Sienna's eating habits (she'd developed a real craving for mozzarella, among other things), she appeared to have lost rather than gained weight. 'It must be all my nervous energy!' she told Jude.

As she fidgeted, crossed and uncrossed her legs, sparked up a Malboro Light and shredded the beer mat in front of her to pieces, he found that difficult to deny. Unlike most women, however, she wasn't particularly pleased about the fact. 'My boobs are virtually non-existent!' she complained, cupping an invisible cleavage.

As Sienna skipped beneath the Rialto Bridge, Jude noticed there was something different about his girlfriend. Not only was she more confident, she was also carefree. Away from the watchful eye of the tabloid press, she allowed herself to relax – even to the point where she'd not bothered to shave her legs for a few days (although she did later confess the sight of bristly pins was making her feel ill). Without her usual hair stylist in tow, she'd even taken to cutting her own fringe – Jude had to admit that she hadn't done a bad job. Sienna continued to reel off several more self-deprecating stories.

'I wish you wouldn't be so down on yourself!' Jude would frequently tell her.

It was a sentiment her best friend, actress and writer Tara Summers, often reiterated. 'She's such a rare and wonderful friend,' she proclaimed. '[But] she doesn't have enough self-assurance. She is very hard on herself considering she is so young and only just starting out. I wish she knew how brilliant she is.'

Jude and Sienna would often spend their spare time exploring the city's shadowy backstreets or stopping to admire how beautifully the evening sun reflected from the water, giving the whole place a warm and almost iridescent glow. Registering the peace and quiet around her, Sienna often lamented that life couldn't be this way in London. In a few months' time, she'd have to revert back to her old life – always looking over her shoulder, speaking in hushed tones over dinner... not to mention shaving her legs!

Of course, she accepted that public exposure was all part and parcel of an acting career. 'I think the waiting on set and the publicity are kind of the things you get paid to do. Acting is great and some of the publicity can be great fun. But avoiding that, particularly in England, is fine by me!'

By now, Sienna had learned how to conduct herself in interviews. At first, she had been bubbly and eager to please. Now she was a little more cautious and mulled over her words before she allowed them to tumble out of her mouth. 'The past year has taught me to be very careful,' she told one journalist, referring to her relationship with Jude. 'We love each other desperately and it makes me sad that the press are so cruel and so negative. I am an optimistic person but I would be lying if I said it hadn't made me more cynical.'

Back home in the UK, *Alfie* and *Layer Cake* had both been put on general release. Sienna had no real idea how either had been received. Partly, that was because she was too nervous to read any reviews. 'I'm terrified of reading them and letting them affect me… I don't want to get into that trap of believing them because the work was what it was all about and the experience that you take from it and what you learn from it, that's what it should be about. Especially nowadays when a lot of the time making films is more about making money I'm kind of sentimental and old-fashioned in the way that I view it; it was about the experience, the challenge, what I learned and who I met.'

Sienna hated being apart from Jude. But, wherever he

was, she at least knew she could reach him by telephone. Sometimes he would call her up to three times in an hour just to hear her voice or tell her how the pet dogs were doing, or that Rafferty had scored a goal in his team match that morning. When it was time for Sienna to wave her goodbyes to Venice, she felt incredibly sad to leave. As a memento she kept with her a mask from the opulent ball scene filmed in *Casanova*. The streets of Venice were filled with local mask makers and it would serve as a fitting memory. But the prospect of returning to London wasn't all bad. At least she could look forward to her fix of 'traffic, pollution and Jude'.

The time Jude and Sienna spent in Venice together had been magical. Away from prying eyes, their relationship had been given time to develop. Now back in London, they quickly became to focus of media attention once again. But this time the papers could see something had changed. They knew Jude Law was serious about Sienna. This wasn't, as Sadie had cruelly predicted, just a 'silly thing'. Inevitably, marriage rumours began to circulate.

The *Sunday Mirror* reported Jude had proposed while the couple were in Italy. Allegedly, Sienna had phoned several of her pals to say, 'I'm the happiest girl in the world!' Sienna quickly denied the story and claimed to have no idea where they'd come from. Obviously someone had the wrong end of the stick! Jude reacted a little more strongly. He was furious: 'There's nothing more uncomfortable than being very happy and very much together and then receiving endless phone calls from the family and the press, saying "Well done", because you have to deny it,' he said.

But while the rumours weren't incorrect, Sienna certainly didn't have an aversion to marriage. Even though her parents had divorced during her childhood, she was a desperate romantic and still dreamed of a fairytale wedding. 'I want to get married one day, have kids, be in love, have the perfect husband, be the perfect wife, make great films. But I'm not going to go there yet,' she once said of her ambitions. As it turned out, however, her dreams would become a reality much sooner than she'd imagined.

The streets outside Jude's Primrose Hill flat were eerily silent. In the past hour, only two cars had passed by. Sienna opened her eyes and yawned, before preparing to turn over and go back to seep. It must be about 6am, she thought to herself, far too early to be getting up. But, as she rolled over, she caught a glimpse of the clock radio. It was almost ten! It was Christmas Day and Sienna had so much do to. Stirred by the whirring of mental cogs, Jude woke up. The pair kissed and wished each other a Happy Christmas. But, before Sienna could get up and prepare breakfast, Jude pulled her back. There was something he needed to discuss with her. For a moment Sienna was alarmed. What on earth could be so important to delay their Christmas breakfast? But, before Sienna had a chance to appear disgruntled, he produced a small jewellery box. Handing it to Sienna, he asked, 'Will you marry me?' She opened the box to reveal a £20,000 diamond-encrusted ring. Sienna was in shock, but with only a moment's hesitation she flung her arms around him and screamed back, 'Yes!'

Sienna felt dazed and drunk on happiness. The merry-go-round she'd been riding for the last few months had suddenly gone into overdrive. So many thoughts were running through her head, but one thing was clear – she was now set to marry the man of her dreams.

Unfortunately, the couple weren't able to stay in bed for long. Jude was due to spend Christmas lunch with Sadie and the kids, who had rented a cottage in the Cotswolds for the holiday period. He arrived and distributed presents, but made no mention of the engagement. That evening, Jude and eight-year-old Rafferty drove back to London. Raff had always been close to Sienna and Jude was dying to break the news to him. He was also eager to see how his son might react. After all, his children's happiness was just as important as his own – if not more so. Rather than skirting around the issue, he told Raff straight out that he and Sienna would be getting married. Much to his relief, Raff was delighted.

That evening, Rafferty spoke to his mother Sadie over the phone. She asked him how his day had been. 'Dad's got engaged to Sienna,' he told her. Allegedly, a fierce row between Jude and Sadie ensued. According to friends, who later retold the story, she was apparently annoyed not by the news itself but the manner in which she had been informed. Later, however, she would snipe, 'It's odd, I think, to get engaged to somebody when you're not divorced,' in reference to the fact that she and Jude were yet to agree on a divorce settlement. But Jude refused to let the argument ruin his happy day. The next morning, he and Sienna jetted off to the Seychelles for a romantic break.

But, when Jude and Sienna's publicist Ciara Parks announced the news publicly, she gave a very different version of events. 'It's true they are engaged. Jude bought Sienna a big cluster diamond ring,' she told papers. 'They've told their families the news and they're thrilled, as are Jude's kids. They love Sienna and can't wait for the wedding.' She added that no date had yet been set, and that would very much depend on their respective filming schedules. Days later, a markedly more gracious Sadie was quoted in the *Sun* as saying, 'I'm delighted for Jude and Sienna and wish them all the best for the future.'

As soon as Sienna and Jude returned from their blissful break, they set to work on making arrangements for the wedding. According to one newspaper report, Sienna was planning to book three venues for the big day as a clever ruse to confuse the media. 'One is in LA and two are island ceremonies – one is in Fiji,' revealed an insider. 'They'll tell family and friends at the last minute.' Sienna's mum Jo set even more tongues wagging when she confirmed the ceremony would take place in an exotic location. 'It will be a quiet, intimate day, somewhere exotic and miles away from anywhere so no one can find them. Yes, there will be close friends and family and it will be one hell of a party –

but they deserve it,' she told the *Mirror* newspaper. Apparently, Jude had set his sights on having a small family ceremony on the beautiful Italian island of Ischia, not far from the Amalfi coast. An insider reported the couple had made enquiries about holding the service in a castle.

Of course, one of the biggest question marks hanging over the day was who would design Sienna's dress. Rumours were rife in the fashion industry. 'Everyone is desperate to dress Sienna – she has been the style icon of 2004,' said one insider. 'It would do wonders for their reputations and of course everyone is offering to create the most amazing frock for her.'

Eventually, Sienna put an end to the whispers by announcing that Matthew Williamson would have the monopoly on designing her gown, but the design details were still to be confirmed. One source suggested it would be 'a classic and simple white or ivory gown to go with the big white wedding she always dreamed of'. Sienna was also spotted window shopping in some of London's most exclusive jewellers, looking for a wedding ring to rival the fantastic engagement ring Jude had already presented her with.

Although the couple refused to announce a date, 2005 looked set to be a good year. In July, Jude and Sadie finally reached an out-of-court agreement over their divorce settlement, almost two years since they'd called it quits on their six-year marriage. Just three days after the case at London's High Court had begun, Jude and Sadie made a civilised agreement over the phone. Sadie would receive the marital home in Primrose Hill, a lump sum of £5 million (half what she'd originally demanded) and regular payments for the couple's three children. 'Sadie is pretty happy about the agreement – they both are,' a friend admitted. 'The most important thing for her is that she has kept the house. She knows that she will be financially secure – although she will still have to work. Jude is relieved, too. Sadie had been trying to get a lot more money out of him. Both of them are now hoping to put this behind them and get on with their lives with their new partners.' At last, the final obstacle in Jude and Sienna's marriage plans had been removed. He was now divorced. What else could stand in their way?

TEN

The First Cracks Appear

WHILE their personal lives were a hot topic of tabloid speculation, professionally Jude and Sienna were also becoming a force to be reckoned with. Sienna was tipped to be tomorrow's bright young star, while in 2004 alone Jude had a whopping six films to his name. He'd also received nominations at both the Baftas and the Academy Awards. In December, he had signed up to work on a remake of the 1949 Oscar-winning political drama *All The King's Men*. Directed by Steve Zaillian (who wrote the screenplay for *Gangs of New York*), the film would also star Sean Penn and Kate Winslet. Jude had been cast as reporter Jack Burden.

Despite having worked desperately hard for the first half

of 2004, Jude had taken the latter half to relax. Now he was gearing up for another big stint of work, which would involve him working on location in Louisiana for quite some time. Having just returned from Venice, Sienna wasn't looking forward to another period of separation – this time from her fiancé. But she'd also come to accept that, if she and Jude were to enjoy successful careers, then a long-distance relationship was inevitable.

After spending Christmas and New Year with Sienna, Jude flew back to America to resume filming. The couple shared a tearful farewell. Strangely enough, even though Jude had shown commitment to Sienna by asking for her hand in marriage, she now felt even more reluctant to let him go. Looking into her glazed eyes, Jude promised his emotional wife-to-be that they would speak daily on the phone and that she should come and visit him within the next few weeks. Nodding her head in agreement, she gave him one final hug before he left. Gripping tightly, she didn't want to let go. Unable to fight back the tears any longer, Sienna began to sob quietly. A small, damp patch of mascara formed on the shoulder of Jude's freshly ironed linen shirt. He didn't mind. No woman had ever shown so much devotion towards him. Suddenly, he was struck by the sheer beauty of the moment. Willing it to last forever, he didn't dare to move a muscle. Eventually, however, the impatient bleating of a taxi horn forced the love-struck couple to separate.

Sienna didn't wait long to take Jude up on his offer of a

visit. Within days, she was on the phone to book her first flight to New Orleans. 'I love Jude so much and I want to marry him!' she told friends. 'Our wedding will be the happiest day of our lives. It still feels like a whirlwind romance because I can't believe what's happening to me. We are both very happy and it's nice to be part of his life.' No one doubted the sincerity of her convictions. She would go to any lengths to be with Jude – even if it did involve flying halfway round the world. She was also quick to defend Jude in the press. During his divorce battle with Sadie, he'd been painted as a po-faced misery, permanently locked in a thunderous glare. That image couldn't be further from the truth. The Jude whom Sienna knew was a warm and kind-hearted man. In a bid to distinguish her fiancé from his misrepresentation in the press, on occasion she would even address him by his real first name, David. 'He's one of the nicest, most caring men I've ever met. He has a great heart and soul. He's very shy in public, but behind closed doors he's funny, intelligent, good-looking and to me that's the real Jude,' she insisted.

Sienna went out to visit Jude on several occasions. But, while spending time with Jude was fantastic, leaving him again was unbearably hard. Often, Jude would spend long days on set filming, but Sienna didn't really mind. She would see him in the evening. One time, she even travelled with her pet dogs Porgy and Bess to keep her company. Whenever Jude was filming, she would take the terriers for long walks in the park. They too missed their 'daddy' and were ecstatic to see him again. Jude would also travel back to London with Sienna whenever he was granted a break. Without a care in the world, the couple were spotted canoodling on a British Airways plane.

The couple certainly painted a blissful picture, but it was an image not everyone was quite so eager to buy into. With Jude out of the immediate picture, the tabloids began to speculate on whether his relationship with Sienna could last the distance. After all, work commitments and long periods spent away from home had been cited as the cause of his previous marital breakdown. The papers also became curious as to why Jude and Sienna hadn't announced a date for their wedding. For lack of any stories to print, they began to suggest the relationship had hit troubled waters. First, they alleged Jude had postponed arrangements, then Sienna had thrown a spanner in the works and finally the whole thing was off. Then Jude created even more of a stir by saying, 'We could be engaged for years. If we do wed, it will be well away from the press.' The ambiguity of his remark set tongues wagging. Perhaps Jude wasn't quite the committed boyfriend he appeared to be?

Irritated by a constant stream of misinformation, Sienna decided to set the record straight. 'We are happily engaged, it was never our intention to get married immediately and, contrary to allegations that we spent weeks apart, I've spent three months of this year with Jude in New Orleans,' she fumed. She also added that, as both her sister and Jude's sister had weddings planned that year, they didn't want to overshadow any celebrations. 'My sister and Jude's sister are both getting married this year. There's no rush, we're just happy to be engaged.'

But stories of discord continued to flood the tabloid pages. Things came to a head at the Baftas in February. Sienna Miller's footloose and fancy-free behaviour provided enough tabloid fodder to suggest there might be trouble in paradise. Busy filming *All the King's Men* in Louisiana, Jude was unable to attend the ceremony. Organisers had invited Sienna to co-present the award for Best Visual Effects with Christian Slater, in London's Leicester Square. Sienna was looking forward to the event and a chance to let her hair down. She selected an Alexander McQueen retro-patterned floor-length dress especially for the occasion.

After the awards ceremony had ended, guests were whisked to the Sanderson Hotel for a Miramax after-party. Sienna quickly acquainted herself with the stars of *The Motorcycle Diaries*, Gael García Bernal and Rodrigo De la Serna. The trio hit it off instantly and were inseparable for most of the night. Once the party ended at 2am, Sienna was in no way ready to return home. She was having a fantastic time. She suggested the group all head out to west London club Boujis. On her recommendation, they all jumped in a cab. Once in the club, the group hooked up with Leonardo DiCaprio. According to onlookers, Sienna spent the whole evening shifting between Gael and Rodrigo's knees, chatting, laughing and flirting outrageously. Fuelled by booze, Sienna was clearly on a mission to party the night away. Once the club closed, she and the group continued their drinking back at the Covent Garden Hotel. After a 16-hour drinking marathon, Sienna eventually crawled home at 8.30am.

The following morning, Sienna woke up to find pictures of herself and Gael in the newspapers beneath a headline suggesting they were having an affair. Unable to watch over his fiancée, Jude had allegedly sent Sienna several texts urging her to go home directly after the ceremony, which she chose to ignore. Reports suggested Jude was worried about her hedonistic behaviour and concerned she was turning into his ex-wife Sadie Frost. Sienna's publicist issued a statement to say that Gael and Sienna were simply good friends. As far as the young actress was concerned, she was just having a bit of fun.

Clearly on a roll, Sienna hit the party circuit – and the headlines – when she attended Matthew Williamson's fashion show at London's Kabaret Club. The designer had adopted Sienna as his muse and the pair got on famously. (Ironically, his former fashion darling had been Sadie Frost.) According to a source, Sienna spent the night dancing, hugging and joking around with Matthew. At one point she even flashed her knickers playfully at the gay designer. It was just the sort of behaviour people had come to expect from Sadie. One report even suggested she'd bent Matthew over the bar and simulated sex, before leaping off a sofa and playing air guitar. By all accounts, it was a riotous party.

Dismayed, Jude apparently made several phone calls to Sienna begging her to curb her hedonistic activity. Some papers even alleged Jude had demanded Sienna fly out to New York so they could discuss the matter. An insider revealed, 'Jude was under pressure last week in America and wanted to talk to Sienna. But each time he called, she was out. He isn't happy about it.' It was also rumoured that Jude had signed on to do Anthony Minghella's new film, *Breaking and Entering*, largely because most of it would be filmed in London, allowing him to keep a closer eye on Sienna.

It wasn't only Sienna's party antics that were causing Jude unrest. According to reports, he was also beginning to resent Sienna's status as a style icon– an all-too-familiar reminder of his fashion-savvy ex-wife. 'He really hates all that stuff,' said a source close to the couple. 'He thinks it is pathetic – that's the word he uses. He doesn't want to spend his life being pictured in *Vogue* and turning up at style awards. He doesn't like Sienna doing interviews with the style press, but she likes all that. Her sister is a designer and she's really into clothes, too, but he loathes it. It's too much of a replay of Sadie – that's her territory and he detests that fashion crowd.' The source went on to say that Jude was concerned about the impact it would have on Sienna's career and his own. 'He has told her to stay out of it. He wants to live in a different environment far away from the Kate Mosses of this world.'

But Jude hit out against the reports by issuing a statement from his publicist. 'Jude is not unhappy with

Sienna's lifestyle. They are very happy and are still planning to marry.'

Regardless of problems in his personal life, Jude had plenty of issues to contend with professionally. Up until now, things had been going well for him in America and he was slowly being accepted as a Hollywood heavyweight. However, a setback to those advances took place at the 77th Academy Awards ceremony. Jude had been nominated for an Oscar in the Best Actor category for his performance in *Cold Mountain*. He was up against his *All The King's Men* co-star Sean Penn, who eventually won the Oscar for his performance in *Mystic River*. Jude graciously agreed his co-star deserved the award. 'I've always loved Sean Penn's work,' he told reporters.

But, while an Oscar loss did little to dent his career, remarks from the awards host, comedian Chris Rock, proved to be much more damaging. Rock had been selected by organisers to give the ceremony a little more edge. But no one was quite prepared for the embarrassing faux pas he had in store. Attempting to crack a joke about Jude's overnight ubiquitous Hollywood presence, he said, 'You want Tom Cruise and all you can get is Jude Law?' inferring the actor was a low-budget substitute. Later, he added, 'Even the movie he's not acting in, if you look at the credits, he made cupcakes or something. He's gay, he's straight, he's American, he's British... If you can't get a star, wait.' And finally, 'Who is this Jude Law?'

When collecting his Oscar, Sean Penn chose the

opportunity to stand up for his friend and co-star. 'In reference to our host's question,' he said, 'Jude Law is one of our finest actors.'

After the ceremony, Chris Rock defended his remarks by saying, 'It's just a joke. Jude Law probably made a scillion [sic] dollars this year. I would never hit a person that's down. Jude Law's fine.'

By all accounts, however, Jude was not fine. He had just been derided in front of 40 million people and he didn't enjoy being the butt of everybody's joke. Shortly afterwards, Jude left his agent Josh Lieberman at the powerful Creative Artists Agency and instead signed up with Patrick Whitesell from rivals Endeavour, in a bid to be taken more seriously. The tabloids were eager to criticise Jude for his lack of humour. They also pointed out that several of his most recent movies had been box-office turkeys. Taking only £20 million at the box office, but costing almost twice that to make, *Alfie* was considered a disaster. A similar fate had befallen *Sky Captain and the World of Tomorrow*, which took only an estimated 50 per cent of its original £40-million cost. Finally, *I Heart Huckabees* took just £5 million in four weeks, despite costing £11 million to make. Several critics argued Jude Law simply wasn't a strong enough actor to carry a film alone. So, when the press remarked Jude had a face like thunder, there was probably good reason why.

Unfortunately, that wasn't to be the last of Jude's embarrassments. Several weeks later, snaps of the actor butt-naked surfaced on the internet. The pictures were taken outside Jude's parents' house in France. Concealed by the bushes, a long-lens photographer had managed to photograph Jude changing into his swimming trunks – and, by all accounts, his manhood appeared to be less than impressive. His temper was also exposed. His spokesperson pleaded with the press to give the poor actor a break. But his critics would dine out on material like this for months.

Following the Oscar incident, both the public, and presumably Sienna, had seen a different side to Jude. Whispers suggested this new part of his personality hadn't been met with approval. 'Jude's not the man she thought he was,' a friend said. 'She was very starry-eyed about him at first, but that's well and truly worn off. They have been apart for months now, and she's fed up.' The *Daily Mail* even hinted Sienna had been making use of ex-boyfriend David Neville's shoulder to cry on. 'Dave is Sienna's first love and she will never forget him,' said their source. 'They have been on the phone a lot over the past few weeks. He is very gentle and down to earth – very different from Jude, who is quite controlling and serious. Dave makes her laugh and encourages her not to take life so seriously.' To make matters worse, Sienna had even been spotted out and about minus her ostentatious engagement ring.

In light of so many reports, acquaintances began to voice doubts that the relationship would ultimately work. 'They met on a film set and in my opinion if Sienna had been a bit more experienced she would have left the liaison there,' said one. 'Movie people are always having onset romances and most are just left to die once the shooting finishes. I don't think she needs him – he's complicated and she's just a fresh, lovely young girl.' Another added, 'I personally don't see them making it up the aisle. She's just too young. I think she will fall for someone else and that will be it.' One of Jude's circle, who refused to be named, explained that most of the problems in the relationship had arisen because Jude had always leaned on Sienna for support. In the past, Sadie had commented that, when stressed, Jude could be bossy and bullying.

Fed up with all the ambiguity surrounding the relationship, Jude's publicist, Ciara Parkes, quickly issued a statement. 'They are not on the rocks at all. They could not be happier. If things were rocky then I would keep my mouth shut, but they are not. Jude is just about to finish his film and Sienna is doing a play over here this summer, so they are going to be together in a few weeks' time for the rest of the summer. As far as the marriage goes, they had no intention of doing anything this year. Jude's doing a film and the dates don't work.'

Sienna also later explained that her gold-and-platinum ring had been put in for repair after two diamonds had come loose. The first stone came free back in February, while a second dropped off after a night out at London's trendy Groucho Club. Jude and Sienna were both out with friends at a karaoke night. Eager to let loose and prove he wasn't the sourpuss everyone made him out to be, Jude was one of the first to pick up a microphone. He belted out classics by David Bowie and The Rolling Stones. 'He's not bad!' commented one observer. Keen to show off his skills, the 32-year-old was on stage for almost an hour. When he did step down, Sienna greeted him with a kiss and an enthusiastic round of applause.

Later that night, while perched up against a bar, the couple were caught whispering sweet nothings to each other. A mutual friend wandered over and asked if they could see Sienna's infamous antique sparkler. Happy to oblige, Sienna held her hand proudly aloft.

'Hang on a minute,' she said, taking a closer inspection, and gasping in horror when she realised a stone had fallen out. Suddenly, she burst into tears. Surely twice in a row was bad luck? 'Is it normal for this to happen so often?' she asked, sobbing.

Exasperated by reports of their shaky romance, Jude decided he and Sienna needed a break together. In April 2005, he surprised her with a romantic trip to Marrakech. The exotic and luxurious north-African city had become a favourite with high-profile celebrities. Hotel owners there were renowned for their impeccable discretion, granting sought-after stars some much needed privacy. It was exactly what Jude and Sienna needed. 'They have both been working hard and were upset by reports of a split,' revealed a source. 'They just wanted to get away from London and spend some time catching up and relaxing. They couldn't be happier.' Jude had opted to stay at the

Kasbah Agafay hotel. As the couple left Marrakech airport in a chauffeur-driven car, they watched the landscape dissolve into a biblical scene of palm-covered brown hills and olive groves. The imposing Atlas Mountains provided a magnificent backdrop. Sienna marvelled at the sheer beauty of the place.

The Kasbah Agafay, their final destination, was originally a 19th-century fortress, but had been updated by a London-based Moroccan designer, Abel Damoussi – a mover and shaker in Morocco. Upon arrival, Jude and Sienna were ushered through a columned salon where mint tea and almond pastries were served. Playing gently in the background, Buddha Bar-style music set the scene perfectly. Noticing the hundreds of lanterns adorning the walls, Jude commented that it looked like the setting for *1001 Arabian Nights*, while Sienna recognised the place from several *Vogue* magazine photo shoots.

The couple were given a tour of the hotel. Several of the rustic-chic rooms had ceilings made of twigs and sinks set in wooden enclosures. The desert tents, however, were far more opulent affairs. Four-poster beds were draped with antique textiles, while a giant mosaic bath tub could also be found in the corner. The only downside Sienna could see so far was that smoking was strictly forbidden beneath the canvas canopies. But it at least gave her the excuse to stand outside and gaze up at a night sky, thick with stars.

The restaurant was simply breathtaking, with its seven-foot-tall candelabra, central fountain and monumental

16th-century wooden doors. Jude and Sienna quickly fell in love with their Moroccan hideaway. As they unpacked their belongings, Sienna wondered what she might do tomorrow; perhaps a spa treatment or hammam? Maybe yoga in the meditation cave? Or even a cookery lesson in the herb and vegetable garden? It was simply divine.

Without Sienna's knowing, Jude had arranged a surprise romantic picnic in the Atlas Mountains. Staff spent three hours preparing the feast. 'C'mon, I'm taking you somewhere!' Jude told his slightly perplexed fiancée, before ushering her into a blacked-out car. They drove for almost an hour and a half along a winding mountain road, before turning off on to a dirt track. Along the way they passed several exotic Berber villages.

'What an earth are you doing?' giggled Sienna, now excited.

At almost 6,000 feet above sea level, the view from their chosen picnic site was fantastic. Jude invited Sienna to lie down with him on one of the beautiful red carpets sprawled out across the ground. Handing her a glass of Moroccan wine, he toasted their everlasting love. A chef arrived with trays of roasted vegetables, couscous and a barbecue of chicken and lamb skewers. A private butler attended to their every need. Platters of fruit arrived, but the couple were too busy kissing. Despite the incredible views around them, they only had eyes for each other.

Later that afternoon, the lovebirds arrived back at their hotel for a private open-air cookery lesson. In the evening, they set out to explore the city's colourful souks. They were dressed in matching white outfits. They wandered past snake-charmers, fortune tellers and herbalists. Along the way, Sienna stopped to examine potential purchases. Teasing Jude, she held a pair of gaudy sequinned slippers in his direction. But it wasn't long before her keen fashion eye was put into action. An orange Arab-style gown fell into view. As the delicate fabric fluttered in the gentle evening breeze, she knew it would be perfect. Desperate to test out its magic, Sienna slipped into the garment immediately. 'Wow,' exclaimed Jude. She certainly looked incredible.

Unfortunately, the holiday bliss didn't last long. On the last night of their week-long trip, Jude and Sienna were spotted arguing in a local restaurant. A fellow diner reportedly heard the couple bickering, with Sienna becoming increasingly agitated. Finally, she blurted out, 'I can't help it, it makes me so defensive!'

But, when the couple eventually left, it wasn't with a sour taste in their mouths. 'What a great place! We will be back,' they scribbled in the hotel guest book. 'Thank you for the cooking tips, delicious food, calm atmosphere and beautiful surroundings. Best wishes, Sienna and Ju.'

Whatever the reason for Sienna's outburst, one thing was for certain – her relationship with Jude had hit rocky terrain. It had been a difficult few months for the couple. For one reason or another, the honeymoon period appeared to be over and the wedding hadn't even taken place. Both personally and professionally, they'd had a lot to contend with. During periods of doubt, Sienna consoled herself with the idea that these problems had been sent to test the strength of their relationship. Unfortunately, however, the ultimate test was yet to come.

ELEVEN

Nannygate

AFTER Jude and Sadie had decided to separate, it was agreed they should hire a nanny to look after Raff, Iris and Rudy. Jude was in the midst of a career explosion, while Sadie had her new FrostFrench label to deal with. In the past, Sadie's sister had always been on hand to help, but it was decided someone full-time was required.

Sadie started to search for a suitable candidate. As luck would have it, she didn't have to look too far. Her personal assistant happened to know a girl who would be perfect. Friendly and good-natured, she'd be an instant hit with the kids. In August 2004, 25-year-old Daisy Wright was summoned for inspection. Although initially a little nervous, the well-mannered job candidate was instantly made to feel at ease. 'Sadie was bubbly and laid-back and Jude, too, was lively and friendly. Although they had been going through a divorce, it seemed pretty friendly between them,' she would later recall.

The daughter of an artist, church-educated Daisy grew up in a bohemian and middle-class household. Half her childhood was spent in the French Pyrenees and the other half on a boat in the Thames. Daisy dropped out of college to travel around Asia and the Mediterranean, working intermittently as a nanny.

Sadie and Jude both agreed Daisy was a good fit and hired her on the spot. Her work would involve spending alternate weekends at Jude's house in Maida Vale and Sadie's home in Primrose Hill. Daisy quickly settled into her work. There was quite a contrast between the two households; while Sadie's house was very chic and modern, Jude's place was a lot quieter. 'Sadie's house was absolutely lovely,' she recalls. 'There would always be lots of people coming and going. I once minded Kate Moss's daughter, Lila, when she came over.' Jude, however, preferred to stay home at weekends, spending every minute with his kids. Sienna was often present, but would busy herself with learning lines in another part of the house. The relationship between the two women was amicable enough. 'Sienna seemed sweet and I got on perfectly well with her,' says Daisy.

In February 2005, Daisy was required to accompany the children on a two-week break to visit their father in New

Orleans. Jude was busy filming *All The King's Men* and missing his family desperately. Excited by the prospect of a foreign trip, Daisy flew out with Jude's bodyguard, a driver and another nanny. Sienna also came out to visit.

During the day, Sienna would spend most of her time on set with Jude while he was working. Daisy and the other nanny would entertain the children with trips to a crocodile park and museums. On one occasion, Daisy accompanied Jude and Sienna to the New Orleans carnival and the group hung out together. While fans constantly hounded Jude, Sienna enjoyed a little more anonymity. Daisy later enthused to friends about the carnival, telling them it was amazing.

Only days after Daisy returned home to the UK, Jude contacted her to ask if she could fly back out in March with one of his children. Sadie was taking the other two on holiday with her to Spain. Of course, Daisy said she would be delighted to come. Her last trip had been thoroughly enjoyable. The day she arrived in New Orleans, Sienna was due to fly back home to London. The three sat down together for lunch in the garden. Sienna seemed tense and was fidgeting with her hair. In the space of an hour, she must have smoked nearly half a packet of cigarettes. Daisy immediately felt uncomfortable. A distinct atmosphere weighed down on the afternoon. Judging by their glum expressions, she deduced Jude and Sienna must have had a row.

After Jude had waved goodbye to Sienna, he returned to

the house and let out a sigh. Whether it was relief or not was difficult to determine. Regardless, he was less distracted and more at ease.

'What do you think of Robert Plant?' he asked Daisy. 'I've got tickets for his concert tonight if you want to come…'

'Sure,' smiled Daisy.

The pair took a car to the Beau Rivage casino in Biloxi, Mississippi, where they were ushered to seats in a private, closed-off area. After the show, they were invited backstage to meet Robert and the band. Jude and Daisy both hung out in the dressing room, drinking wine, eating pizza and chatting. By this point, Daisy was feeling drunk. While Jude had his picture taken with several people, Daisy befriended Robert Plant. He took her number and invited the star-struck nanny to see his forthcoming show in London.

Just as they were about to set off on the two-hour journey back to New Orleans, Daisy suggested they collect some more wine. Armed with two bottles and some pizza, they climbed into the back of the chauffeur-driven limousine. Now a little tipsy, they started to talk freely. They were both on such a high from the concert. Suddenly the employer/employee balance shifted and they began to converse on the level of friends. Using Daisy as a shoulder to cry on, Jude told her how difficult it was to live in the public eye. She was a more-than-obliging audience. 'I may be Jude Law, but at the end of the day I am an ordinary guy,' he told her, with a sigh.

The pair waved goodnight to the driver Jess and went

inside. While Daisy popped to the toilet, Jude grabbed another bottle of wine from the kitchen. Life hadn't been easy recently. It was nice to switch off and let go for a few hours. As Daisy came downstairs, Jude handed her a glass of wine. He smiled and wandered over to the stereo to select some music. The pair made themselves comfortable, listened to music and chatted for hours. Jude spoke about his background and his life with Sadie and his relationship with Sienna. He lamented being unable to spend as much time with his children as he would have liked. Daisy told her story too, and the pair discovered they both had similar parents and outlooks on life.

'If I married and had children, I'd want to stay at home,' Daisy told him.

'He'd be a lucky man,' smiled Jude. 'It's difficult being with a career girl.'

'Why don't you find a wife who doesn't want to party all the time and have a career?'

'I'd love that more than anything, but there aren't women like that in this line of work,' Jude sighed, topping up their glasses. 'You're a very special woman, Daisy. Your outlook is very rare, but it's an amazing thing to have.'

At 3.30am, the last of the wine long gone, Jude stood up and announced he must go to bed. He was due on set the following day.

'Goodnight and thanks for a lovely, lovely evening,' Daisy said to Jude.

What happened next would change Jude's life forever. In

her diary, Daisy later recalled, 'He walked round behind me, leaned over and gave me a beautiful kiss on the lips.'

'If you are lonely, come and see me,' he told her.

'Don't be silly,' she exclaimed, a little unsure what to make of his gesture.

'No seriously, it's a big house and you might get lonely.'

Daisy continued in her diary, 'The next thing I knew, he was kissing me – it was amazing. He felt so lovely. We kissed and kissed for what seemed like ages I was thinking, I cannot believe this. Jude Law is snogging me.

'He seemed to snog me for hours. It was just a beautiful kiss which lasted about ten minutes. It was just so beautiful, so passionate. I was sitting on the sofa and he was kneeling in front of me, cupping my face in his hands and kissing me. It was the best kiss I've ever had.

'The next thing I know, we are dragging each other upstairs to his bedroom, kissing and then, in the bedroom, ripping off each other's clothes. We threw ourselves on to the giant bed and ripped off our remaining clothes. I wanted him so much. We kicked off our underwear and before I knew it he was inside me. It was mind-blowing rampant sex. He was holding me tight and we were kissing, it was amazing, wonderful. Jude smelled so manly. He told me that I was wonderful. I could feel my whole body tingling, it felt so lovely. We explored each other's bodies intimately and gave each other pleasure. Afterwards, he lay on top of me, stroking my face. He is a great lover and knows how to satisfy a woman.'

But it wasn't long before the guilt set in. Jude abruptly mumbled, 'Oh, God,' shattering their tender moment. Daisy's heart sank and she suddenly felt used. Jude hugged her and asked if she was OK.

'Yes,' she whispered, before returning to her own room. She tried to sleep, but found it impossible. 'I really wanted a hug,' she recalls. 'So I climbed back into bed with him, we had more lovely sex then fell asleep in each other's arms.'

But at around 5am they arose from a slumber to see one of Jude's children standing in the doorway. 'The next thing I knew I heard the door open and the child was looking at me in bed,' said Daisy. 'I was probably still drunk and opened one eye. I just thought, I am not going to wake up, I am not going to move. I just lay there.' But Jude's reaction made the nanny feel reassured. 'I was mortified, but Jude didn't seem too fussed. I felt that took the responsibility away from me.'

The following day, Daisy took Jude's child to visit him on set. 'My heart was pounding and I was terrified of going red when I saw him, but he was very friendly and there were quite a few meaningful looks between us.' As Daisy chatted with Jude, she was even mistaken for Sienna.

'Is this your lovely fiancée?' someone asked him.

'No, this is my lovely nanny,' he replied.

Daisy felt a bullet of warm air rush the length of her body. She was extremely flattered.

That night, Jude and Daisy spoke about what had

happened. He apologised for having put her in a difficult situation. But when she asked if he was happy with Sienna, the troubled actor couldn't answer. He plunged his head in his hands and said he didn't know.

Jude spent the following day at home, playing in the garden with his child. Watching through the window, Daisy admired his devotion as a father. 'I was falling for him. I knew it was wrong but I couldn't help it. What I loved about him was how he adored his children – he was so caring.' As a gift for all her hard work, Jude had made arrangements for Daisy to stay at the Guggenheim hotel. She was desperate to stay in the house with Jude, but he told her to go and enjoy the break. She climbed into the luxurious bed, dreaming of Jude, and indulged herself with treatments the following day.

It was Jude's last day on set in New Iberia, before the party returned to New Orleans. Daisy was getting the child ready for bed when one piped up, 'Daisy, why when we were in New Orleans, when I came into Daddy's room, were you tucked up in his arms?' Daisy was shocked and speechless. She felt her cheeks burn crimson as she tried to think of a good excuse. Nothing came. Instead, she mumbled something quickly and left the room. She waited nervously for Jude to return home, feeling sick. Now not only her relationship with Jude, but also her professional integrity was at stake.

Jude turned up late from a long day on set. Daisy filled him in on what had happened, but he didn't seem too troubled. 'Don't worry,' he said, hugging Daisy, and they both retired to their separate rooms. Later, Daisy returned to Jude's room in just her pyjamas and they made love. 'I feel so close to you. You have become such a good friend,' he told her. As they both drifted off to sleep, Daisy was desperate to ask Jude what would happen when they returned to England. But she didn't dare. Deep down, she knew it was a question he couldn't answer and that made her sad.

But, for the time being, the relationship continued. On Easter Sunday, Jude even presented Daisy with a daisy-shaped cookie. She was touched by the gesture.

A few days later, she heard shouting from his room. She walked over to investigate and realised Jude was having a heated row with Sienna on the telephone. He seemed really angry. Daisy was concerned and knocked to see if he was OK.

'Come on in, honey,' he said, beckoning towards her. Daisy entered to find Jude sat on the bed surrounded by pages of script. Daisy walked over to the bed and sat down. 'He pulled me on to him,' she recalls. 'I sat on his knee with my legs around his waist.'

'Are you having trouble sleeping?' he asked her. Daisy would never forget what happened next...

'We lay down together and slowly, gently started to make love to each other. Jude looked me in the eyes the entire time, stroked my face and told me, "I adore being with you, you are my perfect woman." It felt so right having sex with this man who I admired so much… not for his acting but his devotion as a dad and as a caring person.

'He never stopped smiling. He always put my needs first and made sure I was happy. We wouldn't scream and shout – we couldn't because the child was in bed down the corridor – but he knew how to satisfy a woman. That night felt so special. I really thought we were falling in love.'

Daisy described sex with Jude as 'amazing' and laid scorn on any suggestion he might have problems in the trouser department. 'Jude was blessed by God down below,' she confirmed. But she also enjoyed the time they spent together as friends.

One night, Daisy cooked a lasagne and Jude sat down to dinner with a bottle of beer. The child was already in bed. 'Have you been in the pool yet?' Jude asked Daisy, with a grin. The pair ran out to the pool, stripped off, held hands and jumped in. 'What would the neighbours think if they saw me here with my nanny!' Jude said, with a laugh.

Daisy would later remark, 'It was far too cold to have sex in the water so we climbed out and Jude wrapped a big fluffy towel around me and held me tightly.

'He carried me into the living room and we made love on the sofa. That was wild, frantic sex. He had fantastic stamina. By then I was in love.'

Just days before the entourage were due to fly back to England, they attended the French Quarter Festival.

In between Jude's busy schedule and caring for the child, Daisy found it difficult to find time to be with Jude. But they would spend time together at least twice a week. Daisy and Jude both knocked back beers and enjoyed the music. They later returned home to get ready for Jude's wrap party that evening. At the party they both drank wine and danced with the crew. Daisy had an amazing time. They eventually crawled home at 2am. Outside the house, they shared a passionate embrace. Everyone upstairs was asleep, but revelling in the danger they could be rumbled at any minute, the couple carried on kissing.

'We went inside with our beers,' she later recalled. 'We were chatting about us and the holiday and how sad it was all coming to an end. He pulled me on to his lap and kissed my neck. We looked at each other and he said, "I think you are so beautiful and special. You are far too good for me.' I didn't really know what to say, so I just said, "I probably am!"'

This was the spark for another frenzied sex session – this time on the pool table! Balls were flying everywhere and Daisy couldn't stop giggling. Afterwards, they wandered back to their separate beds, but soon Jude was knocking on Daisy's door. He climbed into bed with her and refused to go. When Daisy heard the child stir, however, she – reluctantly – demanded he return to his own room.

The following day, Jude said his farewells on set and prepared to fly home. Taking Daisy to one side, he kissed her on the lips and gave her a hug. On the plane home, Daisy was struck by a wave of sadness. Jude would be returning to Sienna and her dreams of sharing a relationship with her employer seemed nothing more than a schoolgirl fantasy. 'I was left broken-hearted when it ended,' she sobs.

But the arguments with Sienna continued. One night, Daisy heard Jude's voice bellowing through the house. He was having a conversation with someone on the phone and he sounded agitated. 'Come home, we want to see you!' he insisted. He came downstairs looking flustered.

'Are you OK?' asked Daisy, concerned.

'I just have a few problems. I'm going out for a bit, but I'll be back later,' he answered.

At 3am, Jude returned home with Sienna. Daisy awoke to a crashing sound. She could hear the couple rowing. Desperate to get some sleep, she pulled a pillow over her head to block out the noise, with little success.

A week later, however, Daisy received the call she'd always been dreading. Deep down, she'd always known someone would find out eventually, but it still came as a shock when she received the phone call. And, when it did come, she knew it spelled the end for her relationship with Jude.

'Erm, I'm afraid I've got something rather awkward to ask you,' said Sadie's assistant. 'Have you by any chance been sleeping with Jude?'

Daisy froze with fear and laughed nervously. 'I should be so lucky!' she joked. But the PA wasn't convinced. Apparently, one of Jude's children had interrupted a dinner party Sadie was holding by announcing he'd seen Jude in bed with Daisy. Daisy hated calling the child a liar, but there was no going back now. Nevertheless, the game was up. Sadie wanted a word.

As soon as she put the phone down, Daisy called Jude in a frantic panic. Strangely, he seemed quite blasé and made light of the matter. Feeling slightly more at ease, Daisy dialled Sadie's number. They spoke for almost 20 minutes without any mention of the alleged affair. Sadie asked her how the trip to New Orleans had been. Did she do much shopping? Was the child well behaved? Now Daisy was feeling anxious again. She simply wanted to get this over and done with. Taking a deep breath, she broached the subject. Of course, she said the whole story was ludicrous. Shrewd Sadie wasn't buying any of it. 'You can tell me,' she said breezily. 'I don't mind. I think it's actually quite amusing!' Assuming she could trust Sadie, Daisy confessed the truth. It actually felt good to get everything off her chest. She'd been carrying around the guilt for weeks and it was becoming unbearable. Speaking about the affair also, in some strange way, made it feel more real. The encounter had been so surreal, on occasion Daisy had to convince herself she wasn't dreaming.

According to Daisy, Sadie found the whole episode hilarious – and had no qualms about spreading the news. For the time being, however, Daisy thought her job was safe. That weekend, however, she received another call from Sadie's assistant. 'You won't be needed this weekend,' she was told. 'Ms Frost and Mr Law are going away for the weekend.' It was July now and the school summer holidays were in full swing, so Daisy had assumed she would be visiting the family more frequently. The following weekend, Daisy received another call, this time from Jude. He told her not to come over as his parents were visiting. Then, finally, she received the phone call she had feared: Sadie's assistant called to say her services were no longer required.

Daisy phoned Jude straight away. He blamed Sadie and said it was her decision, that he had nothing to do with it. Sobbing slightly, Daisy asked Jude if their relationship had meant anything. He promised they would definitely see each other again, even though she was no longer working for him. But that was the last she heard from him. She was distraught. She felt lonely and used. 'Jude always told me, "I love you because you're normal,"' she complained to friends. She'd even imagined Jude might want to marry her.

Once the sadness had subsided, anger began to creep in. Daisy was a problem swept conveniently under the carpet. No one seemed to care that she'd lost her livelihood. She was livid that Jude had dismissed her from the position with such ease, not even attempting to fight her cause. So, when two journalists called several days later to ask if the rumours were true, she started thinking. 'I was really worried it was going to get out and that I should put my side across and my friends agreed. But I was reluctant because I am not the sort of person at all to do a kiss-and-tell,' she says in her defence. She decided to take control of the situation and put in a call to public relations guru Max Clifford, whose clients have included OJ Simpson and Mohamed Al-Fayed. She agreed to do a story with the Sunday papers. Jude and Sadie may have erased Daisy from memory, but they couldn't forget about her that easily. In just a matter of days, the anonymous nanny would become a household name.

When the news broke, it rocked the celebrity world. On Sunday morning, readers opened their paper to find a blow-by-blow account of the affair. One of those readers just happened to be Sienna Miller.

TWELVE

Shakespeare and Scandal

IT had always been one of Sienna's dreams to play Shakespeare. Despite having had no formal training, she was desperate to prove to her peers that she could carry off a professional actor's role. Having recently completed *Casanova*, she also had a taste for period drama. As much as she'd enjoyed filming on location in Venice, however, she was looking forward to a spell back in London. She and Jude had been apart for several months due to work commitments and distance had inevitably put a strain on their relationship. Given that theatre had always been Sienna's first love, a Shakespearean play in the West End seemed an ideal option for her next job.

Director David Lan had been discussing his adaptation of

As You Like It with Sienna for quite some time. He was keen to cast the actress and, as she had no plans for the summer, she eagerly agreed. The production would be set in 1940s France against the backdrop of World War II. Sienna would play the part of Celia.

'Being English, you have Shakespeare shoved down your throat from age four. Not that that's a bad thing,' said Sienna on her decision to take the role. 'I don't know if it's a rule that English actors have to do Shakespeare, but you do get a lot of kudos if you do theatre. I think they don't really take you seriously until you do that. That wasn't necessarily why I did it – but I suppose, if I'm honest, it played a little part, because I'm desperate to be seen as something other than a boho-chic girlfriend. I feel, within myself, that I have a right to be here.'

Sienna was tired of being labelled a fashionista. She felt it detracted somewhat from her true convictions as an actress. Being an A-list celebrity in *Heat* magazine was more of a put-off than an attraction to most worthy directors. Sienna knew she had to prove herself and five months of Shakespeare could be just the ticket she needed. After that, no one could doubt her commitment to an acting career. Inquisitive and ambitious, she was always on the look-out for new challenges. She loved meeting new people and gleaning skills from seasoned actors. 'It's not about being a star. I just love what I do because I'm fascinated with people, more than celebrity. I like studying people because then you understand them better.' Besides, she loved a challenge: 'The main reason I decided to do the play is because the very thought of it totally terrified me.'

By taking on the role of Celia, Sienna was playing it safe. Although she'd done plenty of theatre in the past, this would be her UK stage debut. By dipping one toe in at a time, she wasn't about to make a fool of herself by stretching her rookie skills beyond their capabilities. 'I'm not stupid enough to play the longest role in Shakespeare's history!' she laughs. But, when the play finally opened at London's Wyndham Theatre on 3 June, Sienna was shaking with fear. 'I was nervous,' she said afterwards. 'It could have backfired horribly! On preview night I was practically vomiting in the wings. I mean, really, I was literally retching.'

It had been quite some time since Sienna had performed in front of a live audience. Now accustomed to long and laborious takes in front of a camera, she'd forgotten quite what an exhilarating experience it could be. 'There's something about the live audience – the instant gratification that you get on stage… the nerves… that anything can happen… that things go wrong… that people forget lines or just the improvisation that comes about. It's like an endurance test – you're climbing this mountain. After 20 performances, you can't keep doing the same thing or you'll drive yourself nuts, so you adapt as the run goes on. What you learn is to find different things about the character to change things. In front of a live audience, it's a terrifying thing to do but you do it and then you start changing relationships with each other. And it's just given me a different approach to how I can do roles in the future.'

As Sienna glided off stage, she was on a complete high. The terror had subsided and in its place was euphoria. 'It's a wonderful feeling,' she said of performing on stage. 'You've sweated and you've cried and you've laughed and you feel like you've earned that applause, and then you bow and you leave and that's what it's all about. It's fantastic.'

Reviews of the show were mixed. Some critics were quick to slight Sienna for lack of experience. 'At least Sienna Miller is easy on the eye,' one reviewer wrote, in a rather one-dimensional take on her performance. 'And if she were in a girls' school show, rather than the West End, you would think her well above average.' However, far more positive reports soon began to appear. 'Forget all the fiancée of Jude Law hype,' wrote Sheridan Morley in the *Daily Express*. 'What Sienna gives here is a stage debut of breathtaking assurance.' Michael Billington observed in the *Guardian* that 'Sienna Miller may be a celebrity, but she can also act.'

But Sienna remained critical about her performance. 'Unfortunately, I am the type of person who will never think they are good enough,' she said with a sigh. 'But getting through three hours of Shakespeare a night without making a fool of myself has definitely urged me on.' Her real opportunity to shine, however, came several days into the run, when lead actress Helen McCrory suddenly fell sick.

In 2005 Sienna made some dramatic changes to her appearance. Her long blonde locks were cropped into a short 1960s-style cut, and the floaty boho-style clothes were a thing of the past.

Sienna on the set of *Casanova* with Heath Ledger. The part of Francesca was a dream role for Sienna. It both gave her the chance to prove her acting abilities in a more meaty role, and allowed her to branch out from the modern roles with which she is generally associated.

Above: Sienna with the cast of *Casanova* at the London film premiere, February 2006. (*From left to right*) Tim McInnerny, guest, Natalie Dormer, Charlie Cox, Sienna Miller, Leigh Lawson, Helen McCrory, Omid Djalili and guest.

Below left: Sienna and her co-star Heath Ledger at the New York film premiere of *Casanova*, December 2005.

Below right: Sienna at the *Casanova* world premiere at the 62nd Venice international film festival, September 2005. The rain may have been pouring, but Sienna looked as stunning as ever with a silver umbrella to match her strapless Christian Dior dress.

Above: Sienna and actors Oliver Platt and Heath Ledger arrived in style for the press conference and photocall for *Casanova*, Venice international film festival, September 2005.

Below: For Sienna's next project she moved from the silver screen to the West End stage. She played the part of Celia in David Lan's 1940s adaptation of Shakespeare's *As You Like It*. She is pictured here on stage alongside Andrew Woodhall, Wyndhams Theatre, June 2005.

Only a week after Jude's admission of his infidelity, Sienna made her first public appearance at a Cartier polo match, July 2005. It was pictures from this event that sparked rumours of a romance between Sienna and her old flame Orlando Bloom (*inset*).

Sienna caused a stir when she strolled the streets of New York wearing a trilby and a designer swimsuit.

Above: Sienna's most meaty role to date arose when she landed the part of Andy Warhol's associate Edie Sedgwick in the independent film *Factory Girl*. She is pictured here on screen with Guy Pearce who played Andy Warhol.

Below left: Once again, when filming *Factory Girl*, rumours began to spread about Sienna's relationship with one of her co-stars. This time she was linked to the *Star Wars* star Hayden Christiansen.

Below right: Sienna on screen in one of her most recent films *Interview*, April 2006.

Confirming Sienna's status as both a British style icon and a widely respected celebrity, she was invited to host the AngloMania Ball. The stunning gold sequinned mini-dress that Sienna donned for the lavish New York party demonstrates exactly why she was selected for this honour.

Tired and overworked, Helen had collapsed from gastroenteritis and dehydration during a matinee performance. David Lan was ready to call upon the services of understudy Denise Gough, when he received a text from Sienna: 'I know Rosalind's part if you need me to do it.' David was astonished. After all, there was no reason why Sienna should know a single line. In fact, keen to make a good impression, Sienna had learned not only her own lines but also those of her leading lady. Perhaps deep down she had hoped that one day she might have the opportunity to step into Helen's shoes. Just 90 minutes before curtain call, David decided to take a risk and let Sienna take the lead. 'Are you sure you can do this?' he asked, knowing full well she was more than capable.

'Of course I can,' she said, biting her lip.

In truth, she was a nervous wreck. But eager to seize the opportunity to prove herself, she blocked any doubts from her mind. She'd spent hours watching Helen rehearse and knew her role almost move by move. 'I just attempted to imitate Helen McCrory,' she said afterwards. Of course, she pulled off the part fantastically and received a standing ovation from both cast and audience. Stepping into the wings, Sienna was in a state of shock. 'I'm not completely conscious of what just happened,' she muttered to David as he gave her a hug. Later, she would describe the show as 'the most terrifying moment of my entire life'.

By all accounts, *As You Like It* was a success. In a year widely considered dead for theatre, the team managed to extend their run. 'We had our hundredth show and that means I've done three hundred hours of Shakespeare, which is full on,' remarked Sienna proudly. All-consumed by the show, Sienna was locked in a little bubble. Her personal life had been temporarily relegated to the second division, while she concentrated on advancing her career. Admittedly, her increasing absences had caused friction with Jude, but as an actor himself she knew he understood it came with the territory. As for the rest of the world, Sienna remained oblivious. She was soon brought back to reality, however, with a very rude awakening.

Sienna stirred to the sound of her phone ringing. She'd been sleeping heavily and at first had tried to ignore the piercing disruption. But the phone refused to go away. Groaning, she rolled over and picked up the receiver.

'Hello,' she croaked, barely able to get the words out.

'Sienna.' It was her agent and he sounded quite serious. 'Have you seen the papers today?'

'No, I'm still in bed,' she replied, now slightly anxious and a little irritated.

'I think you'd better.'

What on earth could it be now? Sienna was growing sick and tired of the paparazzi. Knowing her luck, they'd probably caught her picking up dog shit on Hampstead Heath… But being papped in uncompromising situations had become a daily bane for the reluctant celebrity. This must be different. Something was clearly wrong.

Nothing could prepare Sienna for the headline that awaited her. Her face dropped when she recognised the picture of Daisy. As she tentatively read the piece, her stomach turned. She couldn't bear to carry on and abruptly abandoned the paper. Tears welled up in her eyes, but she refused to cry. She tore through her memory, desperately searching for any signs that might have given it away. She felt repulsed, physically sick.

More than anything, Sienna felt betrayed. She reportedly told one pal that, at that moment, she hated Jude. In the space of 24 hours, Sienna's life had changed completely. The man she was set to marry had turned out to be a fraud. How could she possibly believe he had ever loved her? Sienna phoned her mum Jo immediately, before packing an overnight bag and leaving to go and stay with her. 'Sienna is probably too angry for tears at the moment. It is anger and betrayal. Never in a million years would I have suspected that he would do that to my daughter,' Jo told the papers. 'We have been speaking regularly and neither of us has had too much sleep. But she is an absolute trooper, my Sienna. She has always been very strong.' Fiercely protective of her daughter's well-being, she added, 'We were really hoping that Jude was the right guy for Sienna. Now we just feel totally betrayed. He's a bloody idiot, and you can quote me on that.'

Reports flooded the tabloid pages. 'He's hurt the family even more than he's hurt Sienna and for that they will never forgive him,' said one insider. 'It's what Jude does. He's good at breaking people's hearts and mucking them about.' Another was quoted as saying, 'Sienna can't face the world. The full implication of Jude's betrayal has now hit home. She's in bits. It's like there's been a death in the family.' It seemed everyone in the world had an opinion on the Nannygate saga – except for Sienna. She remained silent.

As soon as news broke of the affair, paparazzi photographers descended on Sienna. Hawk-like, they watched her every move. She had always hated media attention, but now she was experiencing new levels of intrusion and harassment. Sienna was taking no chances; she insisted security travel with her at all times. The very next day, motorcycles sped across town in pursuit of her blacked-out Range Rover. They followed her into shops, restaurants and even a waxing parlour. By the end of the day, Sienna had 12 crews in tow. She tried to seek refuge at a back table in a restaurant, but had little success. The photographers relentlessly snapped through the windows. She wondered if any of them actually had a conscience.

That night, Sienna was due to appear on stage at the Wyndham Theatre. She was struck by a dilemma: she was distraught and desperate to keep a low profile, but at the same time she couldn't be beholden to media pressure. Dropping out of the show now would only confirm what her critics had thought all along – that her celebrity status would always overshadow and interfere with her professional acting career. Putting on a brave face, Sienna called David Lan and told him she would be present for that evening's performance.

As Sienna had predicted, a crew of photographers was waiting at the theatre entrance. Security quickly bundled her into the auditorium. But, before she entered, she took the opportunity to subtly lift her left hand to camera. On reflection, she's not sure now whether the gesture was intentional or not. It was the money shot all the papers were after, though: Sienna had removed her engagement ring. The wedding of the decade was officially 'off'.

Once inside, Sienna experienced a new burst of energy. She defiantly refused to let anyone get the better of her. For the next three hours, she would become someone else – and that in itself came as a massive relief. But getting up on stage in front of all those people wasn't easy. All Sienna really wanted to do with hide under the covers and block out the world. Instead, she was doing the exact opposite. For a moment, she questioned the wisdom of it all. 'I was vomiting in the wings,' she shudders. 'That was tough. More than anything, just knowing that the eight hundred people in front of you know exactly what you're going through made it tough. There are all these bits in the play when I had to cry, and I could just hear people asking themselves, "Is she really crying?" The first night I was a wreck, and then afterwards all of these women stood up and were like, "You go, girl!" when I took my curtain call.'

Sienna smiles fondly at the memory. Overwhelmed by so much support, she left the stage in tears. 'They were like little sisters and really supportive, but it was also a little weird feeling these people willing you through it. I think that, when you're doing a play, it's like twenty per cent performance and the rest is audience – they give you so much. You can really sense their vibe.'

'She did fantastically,' said her co-star Helen McCrory, who had also worked with Sienna on *Casanova* and had by now become a good friend. 'I think a lot of the critics arrived baying for her blood, and they were totally proven wrong. The play's about love and, when your private life has been splashed over the papers, you're aware of the resonance that that's going to give the audience.'

As Sienna left the theatre that evening, she was pursued by a ten-strong paparazzi convoy. Once safely back at her mother's house, she broke down. The tears she'd been fighting finally won their battle. Despite her protests, it was agreed she should pull out of the show the next night. Photographers returned to their stake-out spot the next day to discover a sign hanging in the entrance: 'Tonight the part of Celia will be played by Denise Gough.'

Of course, no one criticised Sienna for pulling out. It was unanimously agreed that she should take a break. 'I decided I didn't want to run the gauntlet and everyone agreed,' she later told reporters. 'I went on stage on the Monday [after the story was published], then on the Tuesday I had another personal, huge thing happen and I just couldn't go. I felt bad doing that, but I had a very, very, very good reason, which I'm not going to go into.' But she vowed the break would only be temporary. Like a trooper, Sienna was back on stage the following night.

Jude was in the midst of filming *Breaking and Entering*. Ironically, the one time he'd love to be a million miles from home, he happened to be filming right on the doorstep. Photographers quickly tracked him down and kept an on-set vigil. According to onlookers, the actor was in a bad way. 'His eyes were swollen and his voice was husky. He looked terrible and was thoroughly miserable.' Tormented by the stupidity of his actions, he'd barely slept a wink since the news broke. He knew there was only one person he could blame for this mess. According to newspaper reports, his mother had told him to 'face up to his responsibilities and stop feeling sorry for himself', while his dad allegedly counselled him to 'accept that a future without Sienna is a serious possibility'.

While Jude was willing to accept responsibility for his actions, he wasn't about to give up. 'He is inconsolable – not only because of what he stands to lose but because of the pain he's put Sienna through,' said a source close to the actor. 'He understands that she'll want to punish him but he's hoping that they can work through it.'

To make matters worse, reports had surfaced suggesting that Jude blamed Sienna for the affair. Allegedly, Sienna had phoned Jude the morning she found out about the affair, demanding an explanation. But, instead of seeking forgiveness, Jude apparently blamed the affair on Sienna's absence. He credited her party lifestyle for driving him away.

While Jude could do nothing to change the past, it was obvious he couldn't remain silent for long. Portrayed as a wretch and a philanderer, he knew public opinion of him was at an all-time low. Right now, he didn't care. He didn't deserve any sympathy. His only concern was for Sienna. Reconciliation was a long way off, but he had to do something. He decided to break his silence and issue a public apology. He distributed the statement to every major newspaper in Britain: 'I want to publicly apologise to Sienna and our respective families for the pain that I have caused. There is no defence for my actions which I sincerely regret and I ask that you respect our privacy at this very difficult time.'

Jude continued his charm offensive by sending Sienna flowers and calling her on a daily basis. But she refused to meet up with him. Friends agreed the relationship was over. There was no way Sienna could take Jude back. Seeking solace from her private life, Sienna threw herself into her work. What at first seemed like an unbearable endurance very quickly became her saving grace. 'I was emotionally really wrought,' she recalls. 'And sometimes I thought, There is no possible way I can do this. But very soon I realised I had been given the gift of being able to be someone else for three hours at a time. Suddenly, I was saying someone else's lines and thinking someone else's thoughts and it really took me out of myself.'

The whole experience provided a much-needed distraction. In a Q&A session at the Wyndham Theatre,

Sienna thanked her co-stars for helping her through the difficult split. 'There's this lovely expression – Dr Theatre. It's great, it's what I love doing, I wouldn't want to do anything else,' she said, with a smile. It was the first time Sienna had spoken publicly about the affair. Dressed in a pink mini-dress and thick black tights, she surprised guests by joining director David Lan on stage. Despite chain-smoking nervously throughout the 20-minute session, she put on a brave front. At one point, her director put his arm around her for added support and protection. 'Now the theatre has extra security and I just want to keep my mind focused on my career,' she said. 'I am back hard at work. I am determined not to think of anything else. I've had a pretty dreadful week, but I'm bearing up. I'm enjoying myself today and trying to get a bit of peace and quiet.'

Offers of support flooded into the theatre. Each night Sienna would arrive at her dressing room to find a huge pile of letters and parcels from caring strangers. 'Jilly Cooper – whom I have never met in my life – wrote me one of the nicest letters I've ever had!'

Unfortunately, however, not everybody had Sienna's best interests at heart. Locked into her theatre run, there was no escape from the paparazzi. They camped outside the stage door and some even managed to sneak into the auditorium. They refused to give up. 'I've just done a three-hour show,' Sienna would sigh. 'Please leave me alone.'

Several times, David Lan would intervene. 'Now that's

enough!' he shouted, as they scrambled to get a picture of Sienna stuck in traffic.

Desperate for a reaction, they would shower her with abuse. 'Oi, Sienna, how's Jude?' one hollered sarcastically. 'Where's your ring?' called another, firing a round of flash bulbs in her face.

She tried desperately hard to remain calm. Often there would be up to 50 photographers on her tail. 'It's a bit like living in a video game,' she told one magazine. Some reporters even went to the lengths of bugging Sienna's mobile, forcing her to change phone number several times. Hounded relentlessly, Sienna was also under physical threat. 'I've been in situations where I'm running down the street at midnight on my own with ten full-grown men chasing me in the dark, and if you take away the cameras what have you got? I'm a young girl being chased by ten full-grown men, and that should not be allowed, so I feel very threatened by that.'

For the most part, Sienna refused to give in. The more photographers tried to goad her with cruel remarks, the brighter she'd smile. 'I try to handle myself with dignity… it's just very hard to be tolerant.' Occasionally, she would lose her cool and kick a photographer, screaming, 'Fuck off, you fat oaf.' But any sign of emotion would be quickly lapped up. 'When you look upset or angry, they say it's because you had a fight, but really it's because you have fifteen guys with cameras up your nose screaming, "Slut!"' she explained.

Given their persistence, it was only a matter of time before Sienna broke down in public. After all, she was only human. One particularly aggressive photographer trailed Sienna relentlessly and simply refused to take heed from any threats issued by her security team. 'Oh, great! You're back,' she spat sarcastically as she entered the theatre via a back entrance.

'You know what?' he snarled. 'At least I can keep my cock in my pants.' Going straight for the jugular, his words had their desired effect. Sienna's resolve was broken and she burst into tears. The camera captured every minute of it.

In light of the difficult circumstances, Sienna appeared to be coping well. Women's magazines applauded her for being 'feisty' and 'unbreakable', but away from the public eye it was a very different story. Friends and family grew concerned for Sienna's health. One evening, she arrived at the Wyndham Theatre as usual. But, as she chatted to fans outside, photographers noticed several unsightly red marks on her arms. 'The cuts looked sore and red raw and seemed to run all the way up her arm,' said one observer. According to a spokesperson, however, Sienna had simply injured herself while swimming in the sea the previous weekend. 'Sienna was swimming with friends when she was pushed up against a rock. She has told us the sea was very rough and that her arm was scraped up and down the rock, leaving her with scars. She also has scars down her side,' revealed the source. Whether the story was true or not, it certainly demonstrated that every move Sienna made came under extreme scrutiny. For the next few months at least, her life would be at the mercy of the tabloid press.

Inevitably, stories linking Sienna with other men quickly surfaced. Everyone was on the look-out for signs as to whether or not she would rekindle her relationship with Jude. Only a week after Jude's embarrassing admission, Sienna decided to make her first public appearance at a Cartier polo match. After all, she couldn't hide forever. At the time, she was staying in the country. Her mother Jo had suggested a retreat from London would do her good. Having packed only lightly, she had nothing to wear for the event. 'She borrowed from her friend's closet a black skirt and wore it around her boobs with a cardigan from the dressing-up box and some size 8 shoes with her mom's gold jewellery,' laughs her sister Savannah. 'The next morning every newspaper in the country was asking, "How does she do it?"'

Of course, that wasn't the only question the tabloids were asking. In fact, they were more concerned with the company Sienna was keeping than the clothes she was wearing. It just so happened that Sienna's old flame Orlando Bloom was attending the same event. Long-lens shots showed the pair hugging and laughing. In one frame they even appeared to be kissing. They were later seen drinking champagne in the VIP tent. However, Orlando's publicist quickly rubbished any reports of a romantic liaison. Orlando was still very much involved with his long-term girlfriend Kate Bosworth. 'They've been together for two years and they are still very much together. Of course they [Sienna and Orlando] kissed – they are friends and he always kisses his friends.' Sienna refused to comment.

While Jude and Sienna both remained shy of the press, other involved parties were more willing to speak out. Sadie Frost commented, 'I just want to say publicly that I feel for her. I feel very sorry for her. I think she is young and has a great career ahead of her – but I do feel very sorry for her.' Despite telling friends, 'I didn't see this one coming. It was a total shock to everyone,' she made remarks to the effect that this wasn't the first time Jude had refused to tow the line. 'This is not my crisis, thank God. My life has moved on – I have my kids and my own life to live,' she said with a degree of relief. But she went on to say that she would happily offer Sienna advice if she chose to pick up the phone. 'I have all sorts of advice for her but I do not want to go into that publicly. If she phones me I'll have a long chat with her. I can only give her advice if she asks for it, really. Otherwise, I have to stay out of it. This is something that they really have to sort out together.'

Sadie's very public show of sympathy was not, however, completely without bite. She couldn't resist making a thinly veiled dig at Sienna dropping out of her theatre performance. 'I think it's really sad now that she has felt unable to go on stage because of all this. I feel very sorry that she is so hurt she had to walk out. I will talk to her if she calls me. I'll have to consider what I say. My heart goes out to her, I really feel for her.' Later, however, Sadie apparently told friends that it was only a matter of time before Jude played away from home. 'I was very, very lucky that it didn't happen to me,' she shuddered, before adding coldly, 'It's not my nightmare any more.' In the meantime, Sadie had hired a new nanny to replace Daisy. Friends reported that she had purposely opted for a more 'mature' and 'dumpy' woman 'old enough to be Jude's mum'. Others jokingly remarked that she bore a striking resemblance to the Robin Williams character Mrs Doubtfire.

The second person determined to have her say was Daisy Wright, for whom things had not gone according to plan. What was supposed to be a chance for her to give her side of the story had translated as salacious gossip-mongering. She had been vilified by the press as a home-wrecker and now had a whole nation's hatred to contend with. She blamed Jude for the affair – according to her, after all, he had come on to her and used her for sex. 'If I could go back, I would not have got physical with Jude. This is a big mess I'm not proud of. I'm very sorry for hurting Sienna,' she admitted. But Daisy did little to ingratiate herself with the public when she signed up to take part in an interview on American TV. 'I want people to see what the real me is like,' she insisted. 'Jude is a huge star in America and I will be able to explain how I was left with no choice but to tell my story because I lost the nannying job I had been doing

well for a year simply because he and I had been involved.'
Nobody was really convinced.

What should have been a private trauma was very
quickly becoming a public drama. Everyone seemed
desperate to cash in on Jude and Sienna's misfortune – to
the point where items of 'affair memorabilia' were being
sold on internet auction site eBay. One entrepreneur had
managed to get his hands on the infamous pool table
allegedly used by Daisy and Jude. The sales inscription read:
'It has been clearly alleged that more than "normal"
gaming was performed on this table. I am saying that this
is the one and only table that was rented by Jude Law's
representative and installed in the private home rented for
Mr Law while filming the movie in New Orleans,
Louisiana.' The opening bid stood at $2,800.

The media circus was now a full-on funfair. In the midst
of all this chaos, it seemed Jude and Sienna's relationship
had very little chance of survival. But, if life was hard now,
it was soon going to get much worse.

THIRTEEN

The Romantic Merry-go-round

THE question on everybody's lips was: would Sienna forgive Jude and reconcile their relationship? Nobody knew the answer – least of all Jude. Days after their split, Sienna had furiously refused to see him. Jude even attempted a reconciliation in front of the Wyndham Theatre. Even though he knew the place would be crawling with photographers, he threw all caution to the wind and set out determined to win back his fiancée. Stunned and not a little upset to see him, Sienna made a dash for the theatre. Unfortunately, everything was caught on camera and the only winners that night were the paparazzi. Eventually, however, she agreed to a secret meeting in the Cotswolds.

Jude had begged Sienna for forgiveness. Some newspapers even speculated that he was desperate to start a family with her, in a bid to prove his commitment to the relationship. 'Jude's appealing to every instinct a woman has and he can be very persuasive. He's doing his best to paint a vision of their future together,' reported one source.

Jude spent their time together discussing the future. Sienna demanded an explanation from him. She couldn't understand why he felt the need to cheat on her. Both parties agreed they still loved each other, but it wouldn't be that easy to patch up the past. They parted amicably, but little was resolved.

Then, in mid-August, just weeks after the split, Jude and Sienna were spotted taking a stroll through London's Hampstead Heath. Accompanied by Jude's daughter Iris, they both seemed comfortable and relaxed. This was the first time they'd been pictured together in public, fuelling speculation that the relationship was back on. However, friends were quick to add that, although the couple were trying to work things out, Sienna hadn't forgiven her love rat completely. Jude would need to work extremely hard to win back her trust. By all accounts, though, he seemed desperate to do so.

That said, in a matter of just 24 hours, the whole situation had changed again. Emerging from a car outside Jude's house, Sienna was photographed in tears. It was also reported that the couple had been seen arguing only hours earlier. Jude representatives insisted Sienna's tears were the result of persistent photographers who simply refused to leave her alone. Jude and Sienna were clearly still very confused, apparently bouncing in and out of their relationship with no idea of where they were going. Headlines changed daily, and reporters had trouble keeping up.

Irrespective of the truth, the rumour mill kept on turning. The next story to hit the headlines involved Sienna's supposed pregnancy. According to American magazine *Star*, Sienna had announced to friends and family that she was nine weeks pregnant just days before the Nannygate saga erupted. 'She and Jude had discussed names for the baby,' alleged an insider. 'Now Jude has destroyed any chance they had of bringing up the baby together. If he wants to play an active role in her child's life, she's not going to stand in his way or put up a legal fight. But they will never be under the same roof.' Both parties refused to comment on the story, but were both hurt by the personal nature of such lies.

Prior to the Nannygate scandal breaking, Sienna had agreed to do an interview with *Vogue* magazine. Although speaking to the press was the last thing she felt like doing, it was too late to go back on her promise. Besides, she liked *Vogue* and the journalists there had always been good to her. Not everyone in the media was baying for blood! Sienna agreed to conduct the interview in between theatre performances at the Wyndham. There was a great Italian restaurant just around the corner, which was chosen as the venue for the interview. As Sienna led the journalist from the theatre, however, an army of photographers set off in hot pursuit. 'Quick, follow me!' shouted Sienna to the bewildered journalist. Beckoning her frantically, they took a shortcut through another restaurant's kitchen. When they finally reached their destination (a mere five minutes away), both were out of breath. 'That was one of the most surreal and overwhelming experiences I've ever had!' gasped the journalist, her heart beating wildly. 'Welcome to my world,' replied Sienna, with a sigh.

Over dinner, the pair discussed Sienna's future work projects. Struggling to make inroads into a mountainous pile of spaghetti, Sienna remained coy and slightly reserved. Inevitably, the question she'd been dreading came up: were she and Jude planning to make another go of things? 'Not really,' she muttered inconclusively, staring at her plate of food. So was that the end? 'Not necessarily,' she replied equally vaguely. 'The reasons for what happened are mine and Jude's to know. We are incredibly fond of each other and, more importantly, we are best friends. We both feel that we need some space but, if you've been in an intense and wonderful relationship with someone for two years, it's very difficult to just walk away.'

According to Sienna, the actress Kate Winslet (whom Sienna met while Jude was filming *All the King's Men*) had offered her some indispensable advice during the crisis. 'Next time – if there is a next time – we would try to keep our relationship as private as possible. Kate Winslet rang me as soon as it all happened and pointed out that the only way she has been able to protect her relationship with Sam [Mendes] was by moving to New York.'

Aside from her theatre performances, Sienna had done well to avoid most public appearances. At the beginning of September, she was due to fly back to Venice for the prestigious annual film festival, where *Casanova* was due to premiere. Up until the last minute, she deliberated over whether she should attend. Her mother Jo even offered to accompany her. And, at the eleventh hour, Sienna agreed.

She would fly out directly after her performance at the Wyndham. A car arrived to collect her from the theatre and took her straight to the airport, where a private plane was waiting. Sienna had mixed emotions about returning to Venice. Of course, she was desperate to rekindle her erstwhile love affair with the city, but it also made her more acutely aware of the shortcomings in her own relationship. This time last year she had been, by her own admission, the happiest girl alive. How she'd come full circle! Now that statement couldn't have been further from the truth. Back then, her only concern was to be taken seriously as an actress, rather than someone's girlfriend. She laughed sadly at the bitter irony of her situation. 'I suppose you should be careful what you wish for! Now my career is going pretty well... and I'm nobody's girlfriend.'

Being back in Venice was incredible, nevertheless, and all the excitement surrounding the festival lifted her spirit immensely. Last year she had been an onlooker and now she was actually taking part. Plenty of her friends were also in town. She'd already bumped into Orlando Bloom. As most people doubted Sienna would actually turn up, she had hoped to shake off her persistent entourage of photographers – and, thankfully, only a few of them showed up.

For the premiere of *Casanova*, Sienna chose to arrive in style in a gondola. Wearing a strapless Christian Dior dress and a diamond choker, she looked a picture of composure. Inside, however, her stomach was turning somersaults.

'Was it daunting?' someone inside later asked her.

'Yes, a bit,' she replied. 'But I wanted to be here for the film and all the guys I worked with because they're a great bunch.'

Casanova went down a storm, with the audience laughing riotously throughout. Sienna was glad she'd made the effort to attend, and commented that it was 'heavenly' to be back in Venice. Seeing Lasse and Heath again was also lots of fun. But the real test would come the next day, when Sienna was required to take part in her first-ever press conference.

Dressed in a Roland Mouret dress with her hair in a low ponytail, Sienna made every effort to make a good impression. The message she wanted to send out to the world was one of survival and resilience. Sienna Miller wasn't about to give up. Taking a deep breath, she prepared herself for a barrage of uncomfortable questions. After all, in the film she was helping to promote, she did play a girl who fell in love with a lothario. Sienna chuckled to herself about the irony of it all — she had to laugh, or else she might cry.

As she had predicted, journalists were intent on using the conference as an opportunity to indirectly quiz Sienna about her relationship with Jude. Some delivered their attack with more subtlety than others…

'Venice is the most romantic city in the world. Is it maybe somewhere that you would consider getting married?' asked one journalist bluntly.

'Have you met many Casanovas in your time?' asked another.

'I've met a few Casanovas that I like and some that I haven't and I hope to meet a few more,' she answered cryptically.

While it wasn't an outright admission, as far as the papers were concerned, it was enough to suggest that Sienna was on the look-out for a new love interest.

She later insisted that her words had been misinterpreted. 'I was just talking about the film and the character. I said, "I'd like to meet some more but not in a sexual way", like I'm looking for love. I certainly don't want to go out with a man like Casanova.'

But, when finally quizzed about Jude's affair with Daisy, Sienna — strangely, some might say — credited him in part with helping her get through the ordeal. 'What doesn't kill you makes you stronger,' she said thoughtfully. 'I'd be lying if I said that it hasn't been a really rough couple of months, but at the end of the day I've got a huge support system. My mum, my sister, all my best mates and Jude have been really supportive.' But she refused to confirm or deny whether they were back together or not. Now Sienna had everybody guessing!

But by mid-September, it appeared Jude and Sienna were back together. The couple were spotted leaving the Wyndham Theatre holding hands. 'The two of them came out looking very relaxed and happy, hand in hand,' said one onlooker. 'When they left, she looked really coy but pleased and he basically looked very happy with himself – like he'd finally won her back.'

Several days later, Jude surprised theatregoers by turning up to Sienna's final performance of *As You Like It*. But, at the end of the show, several members of the audience turned on Jude. 'It was quite incredible. The crowd were clearly far from happy. It was rather embarrassing for all concerned,' a fellow theatregoer revealed. Allegedly, several burly bodyguards were required to escort Jude to Sienna's dressing room.

Half an hour later, the couple snuck out of a side entrance and into a waiting car. They were taken to an after-show party, where one guest commented, 'Jude and Sienna were so tactile it was as though there had never been a crisis. Jude was nuzzling Sienna's neck and they were dancing together for what seemed like hours.'

At that point, it appeared that Jude and Sienna were ready to give their romance a second chance. Reportedly,

Sienna had only agreed to take back her cheating fiancé on a three-month probation period. 'He has learned the lesson of his life and wants to do everything in his power to win her back. He's delighted she wants to give it another go,' said a friend. And, allegedly, Sienna had also made Jude agree to a list of six commandments before agreeing to rekindle their romance. These included staying faithful, spending less time with Sadie, not pressuring Sienna into marriage, letting her make her own decisions and controlling his temper. 'Sienna believes in monogamy and will not stand for him cheating. And she has told him that he has to control his temper, as he often used to shout at her and she will not take it any more,' reported a source. 'Everyone is joking that she has written her commandments down on a scroll.' The same newspaper article also alleged Sienna had made Jude draw up a list of all the women he'd ever slept with. Of course, such claims were preposterous.

Fully supportive of Sienna's decision to take back Jude, her family were willing to accept the prodigal son-in-law back into the fold. However, Sienna's father Ed did threaten there would be serious trouble if he ever slipped up again! When the news originally broke, he had been furious and threatened to give Jude 'a damn good hiding' unless he backed off and left heartbroken Sienna alone. Sienna's stepmum Kelly Hoppen was a little more pragmatic. She told the *Daily Mail*, 'I'm sure they'll get through it. Jude loves Sienna and he's really showing that. The whole family can see they are trying to make it work.'

During this whole period, the pressure on Sienna's family was immense. They were having just as much trouble keeping up with events as everybody else! Besides, there were also several other important family matters to contend with – for, while one wedding had been struck from the agenda, another was very much still on. On 24 September, Sienna's sister Savannah was due to wed her fiancé, carpenter Nick Skinner. The ceremony would take place at Buckland House in Devon. Jude had been provisionally struck from the invite list, but it was rumoured there had been a change of heart. 'Jude is delighted Sienna wants him there. He's keen to show her family he still loves her,' a friend reported.

As it turned out, when the day of the wedding finally came, Jude was nowhere to be seen. 'Jude is not coming,' Sienna told guests. 'It's Savannah's big day and the focus should be on her. I've explained to Jude and he fully understands. My sister is a real hippie. She hates the whole celebrity thing and doesn't understand it.' But Sienna was quick to point out that she and Jude were still attempting to put their relationship back on track. The rocky period seemed now well and truly over. In truth, it was only just beginning…

The actor Daniel Craig had always been a staple member of the Primrose Hill set. A long-term friend of Jude's, he had also starred opposite Sienna in *Layer Cake* and more recently had enjoyed a fling with Kate Moss. When news of Jude's infidelity reached Daniel, he instantly phoned Sienna and offered her a shoulder to cry on. The pair had developed a strong bond over the previous couple of years. When it was announced Daniel had been chosen as the new James Bond, Sienna was quick to congratulate her pal. 'I think he's a brilliant actor, very strong and powerful actor. I think it's exciting that they'd be taking Bond back to being more of a misogynist, more interesting than he has become. And I think Daniel has a kind of gritty realism that will be really interesting in that role.' There were even rumours Daniel had asked producers to cast Sienna as a Bond girl. But Sienna laughed off any such suggestion. 'I don't think it's the right time for me to be a Bond girl. I think it might undo the hard work that I've been doing this year.' Besides, she doubted there was even any truth to the rumours. 'I don't know if Daniel Craig would talk to the producers about me being a Bond girl.'

After the split with Jude, Sienna was seen dining with Daniel at The Ivy. They both left through separate entrances before meeting up again at a nightclub. Daniel was then spotted dropping Sienna back at her mum's house at 7am the next morning. Rumours of a romance were already starting to spread. In fact, Sienna had harboured a soft spot for Daniel ever since their *Layer Cake* days – it was something she had openly discussed in public. But, when hit with the suggestion that she and Daniel were now an item, she shot back, 'We did a film together three years ago and have been great friends ever since – and apparently you're not allowed to have male friends.'

But within a matter of days, the tabloids had uncovered a new scandal – allegedly, Sienna had reportedly enjoyed a fling with Daniel behind Jude's back. 'Jude is incandescent with rage,' a source told the *News of the World*. 'He thinks Sienna's a hypocrite for giving him such a hard time over his affair when she's been carrying on with Daniel. They vowed a pact of fidelity after the Daisy affair, but she's broken it. To make matters worse, Daniel is one of Jude's oldest pals and he feels utterly betrayed.' Subsequently, Jude dumped Sienna and once again the relationship was 'off'.

Unable to cope under the media spotlight, Jude and Sienna both fled the country. While Jude took time out in Ibiza, Sienna returned to Marrakech. By now, she was reaching breaking point. Her mother even suggested a permanent move to America might be on the cards. 'Sienna is unhappy with the hassle she is getting. She wants to live a more private life, and she knows she will get that in America. Plus, she knows it would be very good for her career because that's where the film industry is biggest.'

After a period of time apart, the estranged couple arranged to meet in Paris. 'We met to talk about things in some place that was neutral and not crawling with paparazzi,' explained Sienna. However, if the two of them had hoped for some privacy, then they were very much mistaken. According to tabloid reports, the reconciliation had ended in a showdown of tears and tantrums.

The story went that, the night before, Jude had met friends for dinner at La Cantine restaurant. After a few drinks at a bar nearby, the group had headed to the nightclub Man Ray, owned by Sean Penn and Johnny Depp. Jude was later spotted chatting intimately with 38-year-old Mexican actress Salma Hayek. He arrived back at the hotel around 1.30am. When Sienna arrived to meet Jude for lunch at the Hotel Costes, she was already in a foul mood. Onlookers reported that she flew into a rage before slumping silently in a chair for 15 minutes. She then sank to her knees and dropped her head in Jude's lap. At first, he pushed her away, but her tears soon brought him round. He begged her not to cry. 'It was astonishing. Sienna was screaming as she flew into the room but Jude appeared completely calm and nonchalant,' remarked an observer. 'Her face was absolutely puce and she was clearly very upset. But Jude was very calm and within moments Sienna seemed contrite.' The pair then disappeared upstairs in a lift together, before emerging hours later to catch the Eurostar back to London.

Or so the tabloids would have their readers believe. In fact, Sienna rubbished the reports, insisting that her meeting with Jude had been completely amicable. She set the record straight: 'We had a really nice dinner. After dinner, we went to Man Ray – Sean Penn is our friend, and he owns it. Salma Hayek is a friend of his, so she came. I spoke to her all night; Jude barely said a word. And the next day we had lunch. There was no scene, no crying at tables, no nothing. I was there for the whole thing… At the end of the day it's laughable, because I would never, even if I wanted to, go into a public place and start screaming and sobbing. And then he apparently dragged me into an elevator… I would laugh at myself if I had.'

Later that month, Sienna chose to take off on another retreat. This time she opted for a £1,300-a-night villa in the Maldives. Time and space were the only saving graces she could count on right now. She had also chosen a resort notoriously difficult to reach without permission, in a bid to keep the prying paparazzi at bay. The tropical setting was idyllic. Only the previous month, Jodie Kidd had honeymooned with Aidan Butler on the exclusive Indian Ocean island, widely regarded as one of the most luxurious resorts in the world. Yoga classes, crystal steam rooms and ice fountains were all available for guests, along with an individually assigned private butler.

Sienna checked herself into one of the best rooms. Erected on stilts, her water villa had a terrace leading straight into the ocean. Sienna lay on her balcony listening to water gently lap her jetty. Colourful fish swam through the crystal-clear waters, while shards of sunlight danced on the waves. Every day she indulged in massage treatments and a round of exotic cocktails.

But the beautiful surroundings did little to lift her mood. According to an insider, 'She's been sobbing herself to sleep most nights since her last run-in with Jude and she wanted to get as far away from London as possible.

Even though she's being pampered to within an inch of her life, you can tell her emotions are still all over the place. One minute she's ecstatic, the next she looks forlorn and lost in her thoughts.'

As Sienna stepped off the plane in London, she braced herself for a barrage of flash bulbs. 'This is nice, getting off a flight to a welcome like this,' she snarled sarcastically at the welcoming committee. In just a matter of seconds, they could destroy her mood. Refusing to comment further, she went straight to her mum's house. Though, a fews days later, sh was seen emerging from Jude's place.

It seemed that Sienna had reached a decision about their relationship...

'You go in the taxi, I'll take the car,' Jude instructed her as they left his house.

'But there are people out there,' she protested.

'Don't worry, it'll be fine.'

Jude and Sienna were then joined by Jo for lunch at London restaurant Raoul's where, reportedly, the couple discussed their future together and decided to give the relationship another shot. 'It is no surprise to their friends and family that they are starting to work things out,' said a friend. 'It's early days at the moment but this lunch sums up just how far both of them have come – they both believe there is still something worth saving.'

There were even more positive signs of a reunion, when Jude and Sienna were spotted out together at London's Groucho Club. Both were attending a friend's birthday and stayed out until 4am. Mutual pals were delighted to see the troubled couple had managed to patch up their differences.

True to form, however, the gossip and the reality proved to be very different things. Much later, Sienna would claim there had never been any reconciliation in the first place. 'I dumped Jude three months ago. I just could not forgive him for what he did to me. We managed to remain friends but he really hurt me.' It seemed that she had chosen to remain living with Jude purely out of convenience: 'I moved in with Jude and rented my own flat out. When things got difficult between us, I had nowhere else to go. And I've been really busy acting in *As You Like It* and had no time to find another place. So we have still been living in the same house. It has been really difficult, but we've managed to get through.'

On top of all their emotional traumas, Jude and Sienna also had professional commitments to keep. Given the amount of column inches they'd both accumulated, it was easy to forget they actually had jobs to do. The LA premiere of *Casanova* had been scheduled for November. Hollywood was a big deal for Sienna and she wanted the evening to run smoothly. She suggested Jude join her for the trip. The pair checked into the Shutters Hotel in Santa Monica and didn't leave for the next 48 hours. Desperate for complete peace and quiet, they requested staff leave them alone. They even snubbed a star-studded Bafta party to honour Tom Cruise and Elizabeth Taylor.

The pair emerged to attend the premiere together,

although they agreed to walk the red carpet separately. Jude didn't want to detract from Sienna's big moment. 'It's fantastic to have him here to support the film and we're working things out,' said Sienna dressed in a black strapless Stella McCartney jumpsuit. When asked whether she and Jude were definitely back together, she smiled and answered – rather ambiguously – 'Well, it's pretty obvious, isn't it? He's always been and will remain my closest friend in the world. We've had a rough ride. Now it's good.' So were they now friends or reunited lovers? Still no one could say for sure…

After the screening, cast and crew gathered together for a celebratory dinner at the Metropolitan Club. The hot topic of conversation was the restrictive R rating censors in America had given *Casanova*. Bosses at the Motion Picture Association of America had decided the film was not suitable for people under the age of 17 unless accompanied by an adult. They made their decision based on a banquet scene during which oral sex between Heath Ledger's Casanova character and an underage admirer was alluded to. Sienna was both appalled and disappointed by the rating. 'I think it's a pretty harsh restriction when you can go and see terrifying horror films in [America]. That seems really silly to me. *War of the Worlds* was PG–13 and that was terrifying. I took a nine-year-old to see it and I had to take him out of the theatre because he was terrified.' Still she wasn't going to let it ruin her evening. In terms of her personal development, *Casanova* had been a triumph.

Jude, meanwhile, was eager to make a good impression. It took a lot of guts to come out and face Sienna's friends. He was certain plenty of people were still unwilling to forgive him for his unacceptable behaviour. He spoke at length to Heath Ledger about his happy domestic life in Brooklyn. Heath and his girlfriend Michelle Williams had met on the set of *Brokeback Mountain* and had been dating ever since. They were madly in love and she had just given birth to their first child. 'Michelle is just a natural as a mother,' he told his friend. 'And Brooklyn is only fifteen minutes from the city.'

Shortly after the premiere, the couple flew to New York. That evening they joined Sienna's dad Ed for dinner. Jude was nervous about the encounter. He knew Ed was fiercely protective of Sienna and would be watching Jude like a hawk from now on. Halfway through the meal, Ed took Jude to one side. They had a very frank conversation about the events of the past few months. Jude convinced Ed that he'd done a lot of soul searching and was truly sorry for his actions. 'He did a lot of hard work, trying to figure out who he was,' Ed later told friends that if he did anything like this again there would be serious trouble.

Although it seemed their relationship might finally be back on track, however, it didn't take long before the couple were caught bickering in public. The first sighting was at New York restaurant Freemans on a Monday night. On Tuesday, they were at it again in swanky restaurant Balthazar. Jude stormed off and left Sienna after a blazing argument. Brought to tears, she snuck outside for a comforting cigarette. Another passer-by spotted the couple arguing in the street: 'They were fighting on the corner of Spring and Broadway. Jude got so pissed off, he told her one last time to fuck off and then he stormed off. He left poor Sienna standing on the corner in the rain waiting for him to turn back around, but he did not.'

Jude returned home and Sienna continued with her promotional work in New York. In spite of their very public arguments, however, it seemed that things might gradually be getting sorted out in private. 'The dogs are being looked after by their dad, Jude, while I'm over here,' Sienna smiled. Domestic harmony had apparently been restored.

Sienna admitted to journalists that, even though she'd made a film about love, in reality she was far from being an expert on the subject. 'Having done this film, everyone thinks you're an expert on love. And I'm hopeless. I'd love one day to get married and have children. But I'm not quite ready yet.' Appearing on an American TV chat show, she denied her faith in true love had waned any, though: 'I believe in true love. You've got to. I'm not the first person to experience infidelity and I won't be the last. But, if you love someone and there's a friendship and something worth saving, then… he's too close to me to cut out of my life. I love him.' But she was quick to quash any reports that she and Jude might be walking up the aisle sometime soon. 'I can't think about looking after anyone but me and my dogs!'

Once her promotional stint was over, Sienna returned to London to be with Jude and her pets. As soon as she walked in through the front door, Porgy and Bess dashed up to her. Sienna bent down and sucked on Porgy's velvety ear. 'It's like a rose petal!' she exclaimed. 'He's so sweet. Has he been singing again?' she asked Jude. Her childlike behaviour made him smile. He'd missed her vivacious energy in the house.

'His teeth have been bad again, though,' Jude replied.

Sienna lifted the dog's mouth and frowned; she would have to make an appointment at the vet's. In the room next door, she could hear crashing and thrashing. Raff was having a drum lesson. Being back home did seem slightly surreal, but at the same time familiar surroundings felt comforting to her.

That afternoon, Sienna was due to do an interview with the photographer Sam Taylor-Wood. Sam had shot some photographs of Sienna in New York for the American magazine *Interview*. The pair hit it off famously and she was quite relieved when the editor had suggested Sam might like to conduct the interview. She'd had enough of probing journalists and photographers for the time being! She felt a lot more comfortable inviting a friend into the house. Sat on the sofa drinking tea, the pair chatted, giggled and gossiped. In a display of paramount respect for Sienna, Sam refused to quiz Sienna about the Nannygate scandal. Appreciative of her sensitivity, Sienna instead decided to volunteer the information everyone was after. 'I just hope she doesn't run into me in a dark alley,' threatened Sienna. She paused momentarily for thought. 'Actually, I'm quite looking forward to the day when our paths will cross, which I know they well. She better live in fear.'

Daisy Wright was incensed by the remarks. It seemed as if Jude had been absolved of all guilt and now she was painted as the baddie in the picture. 'Daisy can't believe Sienna has spoken out like this. She has accepted Jude back and put all the blame on Daisy,' said a close friend. They went on to describe the threats as nasty, frightening and childish. Some even suggested Daisy should go to the police.

Then the former nanny chose to speak up for herself. 'Why is it that the betrayed woman always blames the other woman, and not the cheating man? It takes two people to have an affair!' she retaliated angrily. Besides, as far as she was concerned, Jude and Sienna's relationship had been inherently doomed. 'I maintain it is impossible for someone to break up a happy relationship,' she told the tabloids. 'I'm shocked at Sienna and couldn't believe how vicious her comments were. She should look at herself and ask WHY Jude was cheating on her. Maybe I was giving him something she couldn't. If he went looking for sex elsewhere, maybe he wasn't getting the sex he wanted at home.'

In the same article, Daisy went on to accuse Sienna of being an immature party girl 'who wants to go nightclubbing and get drunk with her mates'. In stark contrast, she described Jude as a domestic creature, desperate for peace and quiet in his home. 'It was always going to end in tears,' she fumed bitterly. 'They were at war before she even found out about us. That's because they were fundamentally mismatched. I didn't flirt with Jude or lead him on; he came on to me. And, if Sienna cares to think back to all the rows they had, she'll know their relationship was over a long time ago.'

Daisy admitted she was still hurt by the affair and Jude's lack of concern for her in its aftermath. She had, she insisted, genuinely been in love with him. But the desire for a reconciliation with him, which she still maintained, would have struck most people as delusional: 'I think he was the man for me – the man I could have settled down and had children with. I don't want to go out partying. I just want the same things Jude does.' She also desperately wanted the opportunity to explain that her kiss-and-tell was not intended as 'malicious'. Unfortunately, it was unlikely she'd ever have the opportunity. 'I guess that I'm not exactly his favourite person,' she sighed.

With Christmas coming up, Sienna was determined to spend as much time with Jude as possible. Only 12 months previously, he had asked for her hand in marriage. She never could have predicted how the following year would turn out! Christmas Day would be difficult and she didn't want to spend it alone. She even hinted at possible gifts she'd like to receive that year: 'I would love another dog for Christmas. I want a bulldog named Sid. But I don't know if I can look after three dogs.'

In fact, Jude already had plans of his own. He was intending to spend the bulk of the holiday period in Kenya with Sadie and the kids. According to friends, Sienna was livid when she found out. 'Sienna wants to stay close to Jude so they can rekindle the intimacy they shared before their cheating came to light. But Jude won't budge,' said a close source. On top of everything, she was also experiencing heightened insecurities about Jude's relationship with Sadie. Jude's ex had already fuelled speculation about a reunion by telling an Italian magazine, 'My relationship with Jude is the first priority for me. I'm spending all my time with Jude – I can't do anything else.'

It was true Sadie and Jude had been spending more time together since Jude's engagement had collapsed in tatters. The pair had become close friends again and Sadie was readily on hand to offer her ex-husband advice. In March of that year, Sadie had even told one newspaper that she and Jude had split because they simply loved each other too much. 'Ours is a deep connection – intense, passionate, amazing – but in some ways the love was too strong. When you love someone so much that you are in pain when you are apart, it ends up being destructive.' She went on to say that it was a relief to let go of the marriage. 'I never want to be in that place again.'

While Jude's love life had been shoved under the spotlight, Sadie was also experiencing problems of her

own. Several months previously, she'd decided to see a
sleep specialist for help with her erratic sleep patterns. She
hoped the therapy would help with her stressful daily toil
– she'd not only suffered the break-up of her marriage, but
also illness (Sadie was hospitalised with severe stomach
cramps after reacting badly to antibiotics), depression and a
slew of bad press. Her relationship with Jackson Scott had
also hit rough terrain. Jackson had found it extremely
difficult to deal with the whole 'wife-swapping' saga. The
pair took a break to Costa Rica in the hope of salvaging
their love affair, flying out the day after Jackson's 24th
birthday. Sadie had planned an extravagant star-studded
soiree at Pineapple in Kentish Town. But, after enjoying a
relaxing holiday together, both agreed their relationship
had run its course. 'Sadie has just turned 40 and has finally
got everything sorted with her divorce,' said a source. 'She
felt it was time to move on with her life. She's a 40-year-
old mum of four and he's a 24-year-old lad trying to make
a career in music.'

For now, Sadie was keen to direct her attention towards
family affairs. Inevitably, this would mean spending more
time with Jude. But, with the pressures of their divorce
settlement finally lifted, the pair were both able to enjoy a
much better relationship. In December, the tabloids reported
that Jude and Sadie were in talks to buy neighbouring
holiday homes in Brighton. Apparently, Jude had already
looked at two four-bedroom cottages in the trendy seaside
resort. 'Jude and Sadie think it will be more convenient to

be neighbours and much better for childcare arrangements when they take the kids away at weekends. They feel it is the sensible approach to being divorced,' explained a friend diplomatically. Sienna was reportedly furious when Jude informed her of the arrangements. Although she desperately loved Jude's children, she often felt like the odd one out whenever Sadie stepped into the picture.

Eventually, Jude and Sienna reached a compromise over their holiday plans. It was agreed Sienna would accompany the Law family jamboree to Kenya. Jude, Sienna and the kids would then see in the New Year quietly at his house in the Cotswolds. But troubles didn't end there. Further problems arose when Jude announced he would be sharing a flat in LA with Sadie and the kids for a month. Allegedly, Sienna was overheard screaming, 'You've set up home all over again with your ex-wife. If that's what you are prepared to do, you should just go back to her.' Friends agreed that, although it had at one time appeared as though Sienna had Jude wrapped around her finger, he was no longer willing to obey her every demand.

Over the previous few months, Jude and Sienna had both experienced a rollercoaster of emotions. One minute there were smiles, the next floods of tears. Although there was no denying they loved each other desperately, circumstances had made it impossible for them to conduct a steady relationship. Both parties were determined to patch up their differences, but it was an uphill struggle. Friends of the couple were concerned the relationship had become destructive. Some criticised Sienna for being flirtatious, while others accused Jude of being too obsessive. Sienna didn't see their relationship in quite such tumultuous terms. Emotionally, their experience was no different to that of any other estranged couple. It just so happened that several million people were hanging on their every move.

'Most people have experienced infidelity in a relationship, at some point,' she shrugged. 'The difference is this is being played out publicly, so one night if we want to spend the night together, we'll do that, and the next night we may be furious with each other and not, and this is a process of working it out. We both have stuff to discuss and understand and forgive, or not forgive. We spent two very happy years together, and I love him very deeply, and he loves me very deeply. And it's a nice idea that we could maybe work things out.'

With the New Year approaching, Sienna couldn't wait to wave goodbye to 2005. What had promised to be the best year of her life had ended as her worst. But, rather than bog herself down with needless regrets, she wanted to move on. She'd learned a lot in the past year, both personally and professionally. Once naive and carefree, Sienna was now more cautious and guarded. 'I've got a huge mouth, especially when it comes to my business. But I've realised that, if you start talking about things, you open up a floodgate.' The reality of life in front of a celebrity lens was finally hitting home. No longer the desperate 21-year-old, eager to please, Sienna was an older, wiser – and occasionally much sadder – person. 'I don't have any regrets and I hope to God I never have any regrets in my life. Everything I've experienced has been for a reason. And I've grown up an awful lot in the last six months. And that's a good thing, because I needed to.

'I'd always been one of those people who never had anything bad happen to them and I was always profoundly happy. But, you know, you get older and you have experiences that change you, and you come out stronger and more mature as a result. I guess that's the process of life.'

FOURTEEN

Bye-bye, Boho-chic.
Hello, Factory Girl

THE Sienna Miller of 2006 was definitely a changed woman – starting with her appearance. Her long blonde locks had been cropped into a short 1960s-style cut. Gone were the kaftans and slouchy boots and the floaty boho frocks swirling with paisley prints were now a thing of the past. Just like her life, Sienna had completely emptied her wardrobe. She was ready to start again. Military-style jackets, skin-tight jeans and ballet pumps formed her new image. 'I feel less hippie. I just don't want to wear anything floaty or coin-belty ever again. No more gilets or cowboy boots!' As far as Sienna was concerned, those clothes had become a cliché. She'd worked hard to carve out her own image and now everyone she bumped into on the street seemed to mirror her image. 'I have all this beautiful stuff from the Sixties and Seventies that I collected and love – and now someone can get it for like £10 in River Island and there are twelve-year-olds wearing exact perfect replicas of my mother's Moroccan belt. It's bizarre.'

More austere and aloof than her past clothes creations, a change in wardrobe befitted her new demeanour. Sienna had built up barriers. If the past year had taught her anything, it was how to survive. Some fashion magazines would cruelly argue that Sienna had lost her fashion mojo. Once a staple of the best-dressed lists, she now found herself creeping into the worst. Sienna didn't care. As far as she was concerned, it was all part of the inevitable backlash. After all, at its heart, fashion is inherently fickle. Some magazine editors pointed out that Sienna's dress sense reflected that of a lost soul, struggling to find her identity. In fact, it was more of a rebellion; a reaction against the identity tag thrust upon her. Sienna hated being put in a box. 'No more boho-chic!' she screamed. 'Those two words make me sick now. When people label me "boho-chic", it makes me want to cut my hair off and start dressing like a punk.' And, in 2006, that's essentially what she did.

Fortunately, not everyone in the world was against Sienna. She'd suffered several tumultuous months, but had emerged from the Nannygate saga a much stronger person. Her story was an inspiration to women everywhere. In a survey of teenage girls by *Sugar* magazine, she was even voted most inspirational celebrity of 2005. Editor Anna

Brog commented on the results: 'She's handled some terrible lows with dignity and strength.' Back in October, Sienna had also topped a theatre poll for website lastminute.com. Over 16,000 voters took part in the survey, which named Sienna as Best Actress for her role as Celia in *As You Like It*. Sienna was thrilled by the news, and revealed, 'I had such a great time working with a wonderful cast and really miss being on stage. I definitely want to return next year.'

Her experience of the tabloids did, however, leave a rather sour taste in her mouth. It was a topic Sienna had discussed many times. Much to her dislike, the paparazzi had become a regular fixture in her everyday life. 'You see your name on the front of a newspaper, you can't help but look. Day to day, I wouldn't look, but if there is some major thing then I have to read it… in case I want to sue them,' she said with a sigh, in reference to the media circus that had ensued in the aftermath of her split with Jude. 'It really bothers me because it's people's interpretations of you that are totally wrong. You have to swallow an awful lot of pride and say, it's fine, that the people around me know me and I don't care what other people think, but you can't help but care.'

She blamed reality-TV shows, too, for encouraging an unhealthy fascination with celebrity: 'It's reached this point where people are fascinated by every intricate detail of other people's lives. And some people are willing to give up their lives like that. You get these people on reality-TV shows who are so desperate to be famous and they tell everything about every sexual experience they've had, and it seems the more that they do it, the more everyone is expected to do it; actors, musicians, everyone. But I don't want to share intimate details of my private life. You wouldn't meet a stranger on a bus and say, "Oh, God, I had great sex last night, let me tell you about it." No, because it's your business. All this is getting out of hand.'

She couldn't understand why people were so interested in the most banal photographs and snippets of information. Even taking a walk in the park had become a major headline story. It saddened her to know that this sort of rubbish could constitute 'news'. What was happening to the world? It seemed to Sienna as if the whole universe was spiralling out of control. 'You can't move anywhere without having people's personal private life thrust in your face,' she complained. 'I don't know what is interesting about the fact that Cameron Diaz buys a pint of milk or Brad Pitt picks up his dog shit. I just don't know why people are interested so much in other people's lives. It's so bizarre. I'm convinced they've put some sort of drug into the magazines – some incredible marketing ploy that means people get addicted to these things,' she joked.

Quite often, however, Sienna found it hard to see the funny side. During her lowest period, she had even considered giving up her career in a bid to escape all the unwanted attention. 'It just got to the level where I was thinking, If this is the cost of what I do, then I would rather live in some cottage and have babies, because it's not worth it.' Fortunately, she quickly corrected herself. 'I think I was slightly emotional at the time. I'm far too ostentatious to give up acting.' There were rumours that her people had been scouting around the Cotswolds for a suitable five-bedroomed house with a pool, that Sienna was toying with the idea of moving abroad or into the country. It seemed that she had simply become too conspicuous to carry on living in London.

Sienna confessed she was yet to find a remedy to the problem. In all honesty, it was unlikely she ever would. 'I don't know if there is any formula or any kind of way to do it. Just don't read it and just try to live as normal a life as possible! People can speculate about your life. You just have to be thick-skinned, I suppose.' On countless occasions, she'd tried to actively ensure her professional life was not eclipsed by her personal situation. 'I wish there was a formula or a structure. I mean, moving out of London has crossed my mind. But it's not like I court this. I don't go to the opening of an envelope. I don't go to every celebrity party. I don't do that. I very, very much lead a normal life. But, for some reason, if I walk my dogs then that's in magazines.'

Sienna had reached the conclusion that there was no point whinging. After all, plenty of other actors suffered similar problems and they seemed to cope. 'Every interview I've done, if you get me on that subject, you won't get me off it! I'm not the only person who has to deal with this, and I'm not the only person to resent it. I wish that it wasn't so prevalent in my life, but I accept it.'

233

Her gripes didn't just rest with the paparazzi, however. Even members of the general public had taken to involving themselves in her private life. 'People come up to me on the street and say, "You know what I think you should do? Chuck him", or journalists say, "So, Sienna, are you back together?" Like I would want to share my relationship with England. Is nothing sacred?' Sienna was even more repulsed to hear that several entrepreneurs were selling T-shirts emblazoned with the slogan 'Team Sienna'. At the opposite end of court, Daisy defenders could also buy T-shirts saying 'I want to be your nanny'. (According to some newspapers, Daisy had even been seen sporting one of the offensive items in a New York club.) The whole concept of celebrity side-taking disgusted Sienna. 'I couldn't bear it when I heard that people were wearing "Team Sienna" T-shirts, because the one thing I really don't want to be seen as is a victim.' The fiercely independent 23-year-old hated being portrayed as the 'wronged little girl'. The last thing she wanted was public pity. 'I'm quite tough and proud!' she defiantly told one magazine. 'I find it odd that people ask me, "Why did you take Jude Law back?" I don't regret anything!'

While Sienna's personal life had taken a considerable downturn in 2006, her professional star seemed to be in the ascendancy. Slowly, people were beginning to take her seriously as an actress. Her stint in West End theatre had helped considerably. No longer typecast as the pretty face, Sienna was being asked to read for more challenging roles. If she were honest, her moves had not been that calculated.

She had no real strategy or game plan. 'I think, as soon as I did, everything would fail!' she pondered. Instead, she chose to go with her instincts. 'I'd love to do supporting roles and leading roles. Any kind of role with a good character. I don't mind if it was tiny or huge, just to do good work and to grow and to get better.'

One of Sienna's key ambitions was also to 'work with great people'. On her current wish-list were names such as Michel Gondry, Cate Blanchett, Ang Lee and Sean Penn. Much to her agent's dismay, Sienna was always drawn to the more unconventional roles. 'I just want to creatively grow and be inspired. I don't want to do anything generic or dumb. It's not about being the star.' The whole idea of celebrity was a turn-off – Sienna wasn't in this to be pampered or adored. 'That makes me feel uncomfortable,' she shuddered. Her main motivation was a fascination with people. When taking on a new role, she would obsessively research her characters. She tried to crawl inside their minds and understand their core motivation. At times, the process could be draining. That was something Sienna had learned very early on at Lee Strasberg. Even though Francesca and Celia had been challenging roles, Sienna was still hankering after a meatier subject. The opportunity finally arose when she landed the role of Andy Warhol's associate Edie Sedgwick in independent movie *Factory Girl*.

Sienna had originally tested for the role of Edie back in 2005, but scheduling conflicts prevented her from ever taking the part as she still had several months left on her run at the Wyndham Theatre at the time. Sienna concluded it would not be possible to take on the part, but was disappointed nonetheless. Some gossips spread rumours that Sienna had simply not been a big enough name, for it was subsequently announced that Hollywood headliner Katie Holmes was to take the part. The film's producers were adamant it was due to a 'scheduling conflict'. 'We love Sienna,' they insisted. However, despite Katie Holmes's initial interest in the project, she soon backed out. It was rumoured her Scientologist boyfriend Tom Cruise had convinced the squeaky-clean actress that the role would be bad for her image. Katie lashed out against the gossip claiming, 'I declined the role in *Factory Girl* based on my own decisions about the movie.'

With Katie out of the picture, the producers returned to their original choice: Sienna. Since they had last spoken, circumstances had changed and the excited actress was now able to take on the role. Some gossips cruelly suggested Sienna was 'second choice' and had been cast only on the strength of her tabloid worthiness. Director George Hickenlooper was incensed by the suggestion: 'She was offered the role on 13 July, long before the Jude Law story broke,' he told reporters. 'As soon as Katie Holmes dropped out, we went back to Sienna. I always saw her as Edie. It was very painful when she left the project. It's blatantly absurd to think that tabloid gossip had anything to do with it. We cast her the old-fashioned way, because she's brilliantly talented.'

Filming the movie would require Sienna to spend a considerable amount of time on location in New York. With her newly reformed relationship still in the delicate stages, she was reluctant to leave Jude for a long period of time. Both parties knew they would have to work hard to rebuild and nurture their love for each other. With Sienna out of the picture for a while, that could prove quite tricky. The couple sat down and discussed the matter. Sienna was desperate to accept the role. For his part, Jude didn't want to be an obstacle in Sienna's career path to success. He'd been selfish enough already. Supporting Sienna was the least he could do.

The day before Sienna's departure, Jude arranged a send-off dinner at one of her favourite restaurants, Nikita's in Chelsea. 'It's this mad Russian restaurant!' Sienna gushed to friends over the phone. 'It's in Chelsea, near Fulham, which is quite a trek, but it's amazing. You'll love it. It's like old Seventies – all Russian with deep-red velvet and everyone dances on tables and drinks loads of vodka. It's a real den.'

As promised, plenty of Sienna's friends turned out for her leaving dinner. A few tears and vodka shots later, she was having a riotous time. At the end of the evening, Jude pulled Sienna to one side for a private chat. He told her how much he loved her and how much he'd miss her while she was away. Equally, however, he was really proud of her. The couple kissed and held each other in a long embrace.

Set in 1960s New York, the film would follow the life of troubled debutante Sedgwick. A wealthy Harvard drop-out, she came to Manhattan looking for fame and found herself in the company of artist and scenester Andy Warhol, who made her the star she'd always wanted to be, but she gradually began to lose her grip on reality. Eventually, she died of a drug overdose aged just 28. Rather than detail Edie's whole life story, the film would focus on the 'factory period'. ('The Factory' was Andy Warhol's original New York studio from 1963 to 1968, and became a drop-in place for artists and musicians such as Lou Reed and the rest of The Velvet Underground, Bob Dylan, Truman Capote and Mick Jagger.) Guy Pearce had already been cast in the role of Andy Warhol.

Prior to accepting the part, Sienna knew very little about Edie. 'I knew her in association with Warhol, and I knew her name, but I hadn't read anything about her scene,' she confessed. But it didn't take long before Sienna was hooked on the project. She read *Edie: An American Biography*, by Jean Stein and instantly fell in love with the wayward and tragic character. The role appeared to be perfect for her. 'I am obsessed about that era. Everything was glamorous and beautiful and I love Sixties music.'

Although Sienna couldn't wait to style her wardrobe for the project, it was the character of Edie that transfixed her the most. 'I think I fell in love with her from the first photo of her in the book, where she's sort of looking up' said Sienna, leafing through the aforementioned biography. 'There's just something about her... I think anybody who is that self-destructive is intriguing. She had a real light. She was vibrant and fascinating and kind of started a big movement in the Sixties, and burned out because she was misguided and abused. [She] just had an interesting life. I just think she's a pretty tortured soul, but that's quite fascinating in a sick kind of way.' Sienna agreed there was a romantic attraction to Edie and her tragic life. 'It can make being destructive and wild really appealing – the idea of just being completely nocturnal.'

That said, the actress knew the role wouldn't be an easy one to pull off: 'It's going to be tough making the audience sympathise with a drug addict,' she admitted. Then there was the additional pressure of playing someone who actually lived and breathed.

'You know, after you do this film, you're kind of carrying on Edie,' a friend warned Sienna. 'Edie will now be more associated with you than her.' It was enough to send Sienna into a state of panic: 'I haven't slept since!' she exclaimed. 'But it's true. It's a really big responsibility. I should be excited, though, as well as terrified. I absolutely love Edie, although I am slightly nervous of playing an anorexic, speed-freak nutbag.' More than anything, Sienna was worried about making her character believable. After all, it was the delicate nuances of a person's character that made them truly individual and unique. 'It's the voice and the movements and the mannerisms – she was an incredible dancer. There's so much work to be done.

'It's very important not to mess with the facts. But I'm coming at this from a creative point of view. I don't care if ten people see it or ten million people see it. It doesn't really affect me and my job. I'm fascinated by Edie, and that's why I want to do her justice.'

Desperate to honour Edie faithfully, Sienna embarked on an extensive research mission. She befriended former Factory affiliates, including Brigid Berlin and Danny Fields, and would sit and chat with them for hours. Their anecdotes would prove indispensable in her portrayal of Edie. 'Brigid Berlin is fantastic!' said Sienna of the artist and Warhol superstar, who starred in his 1966 classic *Chelsea Girls*. 'They used to call her "Brigid Polk" because she'd poke so much speed! [A poke was an injection of Vitamin B and amphetamines – perfectly legal at the time.] She lives in this beautiful apartment and she's like, "Sienna you're gonna be great!"'

As part of getting into character, Sienna was eager to capture Edie's accent effectively. 'Her parents are from Boston. She's kind of Boston blueblood and lived in California. She has a very deep voice so I've been doing lots of shouting – my voice is a bit deeper than it normally is at the moment!' Sienna had watched several of Edie's films, such as *Ciao! Manhattan* and *Beauty #2*, but she was convinced there was still room for improvement in her characterisation.

Someone suggested Sienna should look up the artist René Ricard, who apparently owned some rare film footage of Edie. She was told René lived at the infamous Chelsea Hotel in Manhattan, long established as a madhouse of artists, philosophers and creative types. When Sienna arrived, the legendary owner Stanley Bard was taken aback by her appearance.

'You look like Edie,' he said with a smile.

'What was she like?' asked Sienna, hungry for any information she could gather.

He shrugged. 'When she wasn't using, she was fine. But she was a drug addict. I remember Nico, I remember Ultra Violet… It was like a cult.'

Sienna asked Stanley if she could see Edie's old room. He nodded and took her up to the first floor. Sienna gently pushed the door open and stepped inside. Glancing around, she tried to take in the space. 'This is where she had the fire. This is where she crawled on her hands and knees…' Now mumbling to herself, she drifted off into thought. Returning to reality, she turned round to Stanley and asked, 'What caused the fire?'

'Candles and cigarettes,' he shrugged. 'The usual.'

It was strange to think that Edie had once slept in *this* bed, looked out of *this* window. Sienna closed her eyes and tried to imagine the parties that might have taken place, the arguments, the laughter, the tears shed between these four walls. Momentarily, she was transported back to a different time. She could almost smell the cigarette smoke wafting around the room.

'Ahem,' coughed Stanley, trying to attract her attention without wishing to distract her concentrated thought. 'Shall we try René's room?'

Not wanting to disturb René's privacy, Stanley decided it would be better to make a call from the front desk. But, three attempts later, René was still refusing to pick up.

'Perhaps we should just knock?' suggested Sienna.

'No,' insisted Stanley. 'You can't go up there alone. He's too volatile.' Stanley asked several tenants if they would escort Sienna. Each of them declined. 'He's crazy,' said one. 'Paranoid,' claimed another. 'Don't ruin my day!'

Finally, Stanley found someone willing to take the challenge. By now, Sienna was really beginning to wonder what she'd let herself in for! 'I'll take you up, ma'am,' said a Texan cowboy, leading Sienna to the elevator.

Once upstairs, he ordered Sienna to wait outside. 'René?' he called, knocking with his fist. Silence. 'Renééé!' he yelled, thumping a little harder. Finally, Sienna heard an almighty thump as the cowboy attempted to kick the door in.

He strolled back. 'Sorry ma'am. He's either not in, or he's not answering.' No René, then, but by now Sienna had fallen in love with the extraordinary hotel.

On another occasion, Brigid Berlin invited Sienna over for dinner. Brigid had been a close friend of Edie and was more than happy to help Sienna with her work. Born in 1939, Brigid achieved notoriety in New York thanks to her famous 'tit paintings'. Her technique consisted of dipping her breasts into paint and pressing them down on canvas. Keen to befriend Sienna, Brigid had even off-loaded several to the young star. 'I've loads in my house,' boasted Sienna later. 'I've got rooms covered in tits.'

'You're very brave to do this!' Brigid told Sienna. 'Capturing Edie involves capturing a very fleeting moment in time. It won't be easy. You don't really have much to go on.'

Still concerned about perfecting Edie's voice, Sienna asked Brigid for some tips.

'Don't worry so much!' she replied, holding Sienna's hand reassuringly. 'You're just dealing with somebody who didn't have a long life. It's the press. They make it out now like she was this great superstar. It doesn't have to be perfect.'

As far as Sienna was concerned, however, it *did* have to be perfect. She was prepared to do anything and everything to make her role believable.

'There is one thing,' suggested Brigid, having racked her brain. 'Edie didn't take off her false eyelashes. She just put more on.'

The more people Sienna met, the more embroiled she became in the project. She desperately wanted to understand Edie's psychological outlook. Taking a trip to the Warhol museum in Pittsburgh, she attempted to understand exactly how Edie had fallen under the spell of the captivating artist. 'It's also very difficult to get hold of the Warhol films that she was in,' she explained to friends. 'So I'm off to the museum where they've got some things I've been begging for.'

Meanwhile, her co-star Guy Pearce was doing a great job of becoming Warhol. 'He's going to be amazing,' she enthused. 'He's really morphing into him. It's bizarre. He's been living in New York, losing an obscene amount of weight, and experimenting with finger-paint polish and hanging out with the Warhol crew. Some of these people are treating Guy as if they've got Andy back!' If Guy had gone to so much trouble to assume his character, it was only right Sienna should do the same.

On 15 November, Sienna arranged to visit Edie's husband, Michael Bret Post. The couple had met at the Cottage Hospital in Santa Barbara and married in 1971, just five months before Edie's death.

'You know what?' said Michael, when he and Sienna sat down to talk. 'It was exactly 34 years ago to this day that I last saw her alive. She went to sleep that night and she never woke up.'

Perhaps the hardest visit Sienna made was to Edie's grave in Santa Barbara. She arrived with a bouquet of flowers and placed them on the grave – whereupon she was suddenly overwhelmed by an incredible surge of emotion. Over the past few months she felt she'd become so close to this woman she'd never met. Offering moral support, Jude had accompanied her and filmed the whole process; *Factory Girl* director George Hickenlooper was stunned by this piece of film when he saw it. 'The footage was so beautiful; I may run it during the credits,' he told the *New York Daily Post*.

Unfortunately, not everyone connected with Edie Sedgwick was quite so supportive of the project. Bob Dylan, who was romantically linked with Edie at one point and wrote two songs about his muse, was outraged by extracts from the script that he'd seen. The plot featured a scene in which Dylan attempts to rescue Edie from The Factory just before she dies of a drug overdose in 1971. 'I have no clue where they got this story,' an aide to Dylan told the London *Daily Mail*. 'Not only did they not obtain Bob Dylan's approval but we were totally unaware of the existence of the project. I do not see how this film can ever get made.'

Another star disgruntled by the biopic was rock singer Lou Reed, an original member of seminal 1960s group The Velvet Underground. 'They're all a bunch of whores!' he seethed, referring to the cast. Reed had been an associate of Edie's and his band had been a staple on the Factory scene; he wrote the Velvets' classic 'Femme Fatale' about her, prompted by Andy Warhol. 'I read that script,' he told reporters. 'It's one of the most disgusting, foul things I've seen – by any illiterate retard – in a long time. There's no limit to how low some people will go to write something to make money.' At one point, the director George Hickenlooper had invited Reed to take part in the project. He point-blank refused, stating flatly, 'I wouldn't be part of that.'

Hickenlooper shrugged off any criticism. 'I adore Lou Reed. I love him for hating my project, which can only bring it more attention. But nobody is making big money on it. We're all working for scale to tell a complex story about a wonderful young woman. Lou will be making some money,' he added, 'since we've licensed his song.'

The research process was fascinating. Sienna found that she was unravelling a whole period of cultural history. 'Even if the film is appalling, the research and the fact that I got to hang out with these people is incredible,' she enthused. 'There's just so much to be done, and I don't think I'll ever feel like it's enough. Some people are co-operative and others aren't. But, even if the film is an absolute disaster, I've gotten to meet the most fascinating people in the world. So I wouldn't trade that.'

Once again, however, the actress found herself consumed by work. Inevitably, as it had done before, her relationship with Jude would suffer. Briefly put to rest, all the old problems were resurfacing. But Sienna couldn't stop herself. She was too far gone. Her relationship with Jude was either strong enough to survive the distance, or it was over once and for all.

FIFTEEN

A Single Girl Again?

ALTHOUGH the UK press were temporarily satisfied that Jude and Sienna were an item, they couldn't resist digging at the fragile relationship from time to time. Reports were circulating that producers on Sienna's new film project were unhappy with the distracting influence Jude had on her. Allegedly, they had banned him from any on-set visits. According to one source, there were also fears Jude would bring unwanted media attention to the production: 'There has already been so much attention put on this film because of Sienna's involvement. The producers want her to concentrate on her acting − not spending time working on her relationship with Jude. It's a small independent movie, so no one can take any risks. They don't want anything to go wrong.'

Ignoring their advice, Jude flew out to Louisiana, where Sienna was filming. Ironically, his ill-fated affair with Daisy had taken place here just eight months earlier. However, his trip was only fleeting. After just four days, the disgruntled actor returned to England. Apparently, Jude didn't want to spend any more time arguing and hanging around waiting for Sienna to finish filming. 'He'd much rather spend time with his kids,' said a source. 'Sienna is also pretty fed up with Jude's possessiveness. They have both agreed to some time apart so they can think about what they want and whether their relationship has a chance. They both realise it isn't really working at the moment because of mutual distrust.'

With Jude out of the picture, Sienna found temporary therapy in her work. Psychologically becoming Edie was one thing, but Sienna was also determined to take on her physical attributes. First of all, she gave herself a dramatic haircut. Secondly, she decided to dye her eyebrows black. Finally, she chose to lose weight. 'If you are going to do that character, you have to go there. And she was skinnier than me. She was scary-skinny.' Already slight, Sienna dropped to a size 6 in just a matter of weeks. Initially, friends and family were concerned that her relationship with Jude was to blame. 'Some of her friends are worried about how thin she is getting,' said one pal. 'We think her stress levels have got worse over the whole Jude thing.' Others suggested that emotional trauma had resulted in a loss of appetite. But

Sienna soon set them straight. A friend reported back, 'Sienna has submerged herself in the part of Edie, who was very, very slim. So she's cut out all fatty foods, including breakfast fry-ups, and is sticking to salads. She's got into the habit of eating less and smoking more. She's not being stupid, but there's no more snacking in between meals or eating several courses.' Sienna confirmed reports by admitting, 'I really wanted to lose weight when I found out Edie was anorexic. In the end, I didn't lose as much as I'd planned because I'll always be a hamburger-and-chips girl. I don't do fruit – just burgers. I eat loads and loads.'

Besides, any rumours of an eating disorder were quickly laid to rest when Sienna attended the Burberry 150-year anniversary party in New York. Celebrity chef Jamie Oliver, lucky enough to be sandwiched between Sienna and Victoria Beckham, told the *Daily Mirror*. 'I was sitting next to Victoria Beckham and she was on the salad but Sienna was getting stuck right in. She doesn't stop eating, that girl!'

And anyway, as far as Sienna was concerned, losing weight wasn't all it was cracked up to be. 'One of the problems I found when I did lose weight was that something bizarre happened to my boobs. They've always been small, but now they've disappeared – they've just shrunk! I don't even need a bra now. It'd be wonderful to have some womanly curves again, I dream about it.' Some magazines even suggested Sienna had considered taking herbal pills to enhance her breasts, now a size 32B. The £200-a-pack pills were said to contain fenugreek, yam root, kelp and fennel seed.

In spite of her reluctance to strip off in front of the camera again, Sienna agreed to go nude for several shots. 'Now I can go back to doing what I do best, which is getting naked,' she joked. Eager to get in shape for the part, she called on her old friend, personal trainer Charlie Cannon to help out. Charlie was an advocate of Chek, a holistic method of exercising. Sienna would follow an hour-long programme of lunges, squats and push-ups designed to improve her core stability. In fact, she enjoyed the physical exertion. So many pressures had been mounting up over the past year. Fed up of discussing her problems, this was the best release she could find.

In February 2006, Sienna returned to London for the UK premiere of *Casanova*. Arriving at the theatre alone, she looked happy and confident. 'I'm definitely single,' she told reporters. 'I've got no boyfriend at the moment and I don't want one.' Although those were words she'd uttered so many times in the past, never before had she spoken them with such determination. 'I know Jude isn't ready for marriage – and I'm so glad I'm not with him any more,' she concluded.

She also took the opportunity to have a swipe at the tabloid press, who had been making her life such a misery for the previous few months. 'I was seriously thinking of trying to get hold of Tony Blair. I appreciate that you are putting yourself up to it to a certain degree. But it's stalking and there should be stricter laws.' Her proposal followed in the footsteps of Hollywood stars such as Reese

Witherspoon, Cameron Diaz and Lindsay Lohan who were currently working with Los Angeles police to crack down on illegal behaviour by photographers.

With Valentine's Day just around the corner, reporters probed Sienna for possible love interests. 'I'm definitely not sending anyone Valentine's cards,' she told them. 'I'm spending Valentine's Day bowling with girlfriends.' Asked to give love advice to other women, she replied, 'My advice to women is to stay single and stick with your female pals.'

Her outfit did, however, draw a few gasps. 'I threw it together an hour beforehand,' she shrugged. Some would argue you could tell! She wore an Empire-style Grecian chiffon dress in the colours of the season – neutrals and white. But she bizarrely chose to wear black tights and high-heeled leather ankle boots to complete the look. Round her neck she wore a long strand of vintage resin cream beads, with a resin bangle on her arm. One fashion expert said, 'It all looks very odd, she is following the trends – but not very well. The top half of her outfit works really well and she'd look very glamorous if it wasn't for everything going on below her waist."

Joined by her mum Jo and sister Savannah, Sienna was determined to show the world that she was better off alone. After the screening, guests gathered for cocktails at the Mayfair restaurant Luciano. Sienna avoided talking to men the whole night and instead spent the evening hugging and laughing with her female friends. At one point she called for their attention and asked, 'We're all girls together, so I really hope you girls will be supportive of me. I mean, we've all been there, haven't we?'

'Of course!' came a chorus of replies. Sienna smiled, reassured that if nothing else she had good friends. They were worth a million men. This was the first time Sienna had really let herself go in months. She'd been working hard on the set of *Factory Girl* and she deserved a break. Knocking back a Bellini, she turned to one friend and said, 'It's been a bit up and down recently, so it's just great to be here and I'm having a wicked night.'

Further confirmation that the couple had finally split came when Sienna removed the last of her belongs from Jude's Maida Vale house. A white van pulled into the driveway and neighbours watched as he spent four hours boxing up Sienna's possessions and loading them on to the van. Sienna gazed sadly at her life, packed up and ready to move on. She caught a glimpse of her vintage guitar. 'Careful – that's antique!' she told the burly removal man. It was one of the first items Sienna had ever purchased with earnings from her acting work. The fact she'd never actually played the damn thing was irrelevant! It signified a moment in time, a landmark in her life that she would never forget. She pondered on how so much could change in such a short space of time. At least inanimate objects would always remain faithful. That much she could rely on. As the van doors slammed shut, so did another chapter in her life.

Fortunately for Jude and Sienna, there were no children involved in their relationship. Jude couldn't bear a repeat of his messy divorce battle with Sadie. Sienna had, however, grown very close to Raffy, Iris and Rudy. She hoped the dust would settle between herself and Jude and that soon she'd be able to visit the family. However, Jude and Sienna had more than just belongings to divide up in their relationship. There was also the question of their pet dogs Porgy and Bess. Both loved the terriers dearly and even treated them like children. Sienna was outraged and deeply hurt to read reports that she had abandoned both dogs on Jude's doorstep. She would never do anything so cruel! Even the thought of it made her feel sick. The article claimed Sienna had dumped the dogs before jumping on a plane to LA for the Oscars. Upset by the claims, Sienna's mum Jo immediately called the Dogs In Need rescue centre (where the couple first bought the dogs) to tell them the stories were nonsense. Sienna had left Porgy and Bess in her charge and they were both in good health. 'The rumours are just not true,' said Sandy Mallinson, from the centre. 'Sienna's mum phoned me last week and she is always very responsible. She said not to take any notice of the story.'

As soon as the couple had decided to call it quits, Sienna had phoned the centre to reassure them the animals would be well looked after. 'They're like our children,' she told them. 'Nothing bad will happen to them.'

Mrs Mallinson pointed out that if ever the dogs' safety

came into question they would be taken out of the couple's care immediately – 'It says in their contract.' However, they had absolutely no reason to believe the dogs were in any danger. Quite the contrary, they were probably receiving more love and attention than they had ever done in their lives.

With Sienna newly free and single, it wasn't long before tabloids were matching (and often mismatching) her with any available (and often unavailable) male. All she had to do was smile in another man's direction and it would be splashed all over the news the following day. At the end of 2005, Sienna was reportedly seen out on the town with Leonardo DiCaprio at the Mood Club in LA. The pair had become good pals after the Baftas. Leo had split from his girlfriend, Brazilian model Giselle Bunchen, only weeks previously. Huddled closely together in a corner, Sienna and Leo seemed to be sharing their condolences. At the end of the evening, the friends chose to leave via separate exits to avoid being photographed together. Sienna dismissed rumours of romance as ridiculous. But, several months later, the pair were spotted together again – this time at New York club Bungalow 8. Apparently, Leo arrived alone and joined Sienna and her pals. Sienna gave him a huge hug and the pair chatted for hours. Sienna then asked Leo to dance but, laughing, he refused her offer. When Sienna caught wind of the tabloid gossip, she slammed reports as ridiculous. She and Leo were just good friends. It was as simple as that.

In the past, Sienna had claimed that it was impossible to play opposite a love interest and not fall (at least a little bit) in love with them. It came as no surprise then, when Sienna was romantically linked with her *Factory Girl* co-star Hayden Christensen. Sparks had reportedly been flying between Sienna and the *Star Wars* actor for quite some time. During one cast party in particular, Hayden and Sienna became a topic of hot conversation. After knocking back a few drinks, the pair were getting on famously. During one heated conversation, they somehow got on to the subject of karaoke. 'I'm an expert,' boasted Sienna. 'I'm karaoke mad! I can even do it sober!'

'Yeah?' said Hayden, a little taken aback. Then, he asked jokingly, 'Hey, anyone got a karaoke machine?'

To everyone's surprise, the restaurant manager appeared several minutes later with a karaoke machine in hand. Sienna clasped her mouth and laughed hysterically. Desperate to show off her skills, however, she took to the stage and gave a belting rendition of Dolly Parton's '9 to 5'. After a round of applause, she stepped down. Slightly out of breath, she gasped, 'I don't know how Dolly does it… because she doesn't breathe in that song.'

Later that evening, Sienna took to the stage again, only this time she insisted Hayden join her. According to one report, she jokingly serenaded the 25-year-old actor before begging him to join in. 'Their flirting was outrageous!' exclaimed one observer.

At first, Sienna dismissed the rumours as nonsense, but,

when photographers managed to snap her sharing an intimate moment with Hayden, she found herself backed into an embarrassing corner. Pictures of the couple kissing in a parked car outside Hayden's Toronto home were splashed all over the national newspapers. In another series of photographs, Hayden was snapped wearing a burgundy-and-black striped jumper and carrying groceries into his apartment. Several hours later, Sienna appeared on the balcony wearing the same jumper, which now appeared a little oversized.

Sienna refused to comment, but friends hinted the relationship could be serious. There was even a suggestion Sienna was planning to introduce Hayden to her parents – a sure sign this was no flash-in-the-pan romance. 'Sienna has had strong feelings for Hayden ever since they met on the set of the movie,' a source reported. 'But she tried to fight against them because it was too soon after her split from Jude. She finally stopped fighting her feelings for him and they have been inseparable ever since. But she doesn't want to get too serious until she has won her family's approval.'

Rumours were further confirmed when Hayden's ex-girlfriend, Lola Skye, emerged to give her version of events. The 21-year-old model blasted Sienna for stealing her love. 'That girl is messed up!' she fumed. Lola and Hayden had been dating for seven years. During that time, they'd experienced some significant ups and downs. Several years previously, Lola had been diagnosed with cancer. Hayden helped her fight a very difficult battle against the disease, which eventually she won. Against all odds, their relationship survived. But after this latest episode it didn't stand a chance.

At first, Lola had dismissed rumours of a relationship between Hayden and Sienna as rubbish. She'd been a frequent visitor on set and by her own observation there was no reason for concern. 'Whenever I'd visit Hayden on set, things were absolutely normal between us,' she told the paper. 'I was pretty surprised when I heard all the rumours about him and Sienna. We had a discussion about her. He denied being romantically involved with her and I believed him.'

But, when photographs of Sienna and Hayden kissing finally surfaced, she had no choice but to expect the worst. According to Lola, Sienna had destroyed the relationship. 'Hayden started to change horribly when he was working with Sienna,' she complained. During filming for *Factory Girl*, Lola had travelled to meet Hayden on location in London. She claims he would frequently sneak off with no warning or explanation. She only later clicked he was spending time with Sienna. 'While I was in London, Hayden kept disappearing. I had no reason to question where he was going. It was only later that I connected all the dots.' Once she realised what was going on, Lola felt angry and betrayed. 'I can't believe that the minute I was gone, he met up with her... She knew exactly what Hayden and I meant to each other. I've been very hurt and betrayed by both of them – especially Sienna.'

Lola claimed Hayden had confessed his infidelity one

night in a fit of remorse. 'He broke down and confessed that he had become involved with her. He said she had pushed him into it. She has a lot of problems, she has a messed-up temper and she is so erratic, she's just not the sort of person I want to be around.' She criticised Sienna for taking her own relationship traumas out on everyone else. 'I hope she realises that not everyone is responsible for her ex-fiancé's cheating and that she doesn't have to take it out on everyone else.'

But, within a matter of days, Lola chose to retract her story. 'All the rumours saying he cheated have blown out of control as we were never together as a couple in the first place,' she claimed. Further shadows of doubt were cast by an 'on-set' spy who referred to Hayden and Sienna as 'just good friends'. 'I worked on the set and I've been to the cast party, and his girlfriend was there,' said the unnamed insider. 'I don't know why people keep saying they're dating but Hayden and Sienna have been really close friends. His girlfriend still visits the set every now and then when we worked on it. And, in those new pics where they're kissing, she was at the airport leaving and they were saying goodbye.' The source went on to say that, on several occasions, Sienna had shed tears over Jude. Hayden was merely a shoulder to cry on – nothing more.

Whether Sienna's romance with Hayden was rumour or reality remains unconfirmed. She refused to discuss the situation in public. Whatever the finer details, it was certainly short-lived. It wasn't long before Hayden was back in the arms of his former beau. In an attempt to forget the traumas of the past few months, they booked a romantic break to Barbados. One newspaper claimed Hayden had finally come to his senses and accepted Sienna was still in love with Jude. 'Sienna's was crying a lot over Jude on set and Hayden moved in on her. But now he realises they have no future,' reported a source. 'So don't be surprised if she gets back with Law.'

The public didn't have to wait long. With Hayden out of the picture, Sienna would soon be back in the arms of her cheating ex. Various sightings of the couple were made, but whether or not romance had been rekindled remained an uncertainty. The hawk-like paparazzi kept watch over the couple. Every day their movements were retraced in the daily press. Within a matter of 24 hours, headlines were old news. Nobody could quite keep up with Sienna's apparently fickle affections. Even the American press was starting to pick up on the stories. Although still a relative unknown, Sienna was developing a reputation. She needed to watch out – unless she was careful, her greatest fears would come true. By this point, there was no doubting Sienna would be famous in Hollywood. She just had to make sure it would be for all the right reasons.

SIXTEEN

The Sugar Plum Fairy Moves On

ONCE *Factory Girl* had wrapped, Sienna eagerly dived into her next film. Her agent had been inundated with offers, but Sienna was keen to plot her path wisely. While they may have been financially beneficial, Sienna had no interest in making blockbuster movies. After all, there were certain things money couldn't buy. Her integrity as an actress was priceless to her.

Her next project was a remake of murdered director Theo van Gogh's 2003 movie *Interview*. The film would tell the story of Pierre, a fading political journalist forced to interview a top soap actress after falling out with his editor. Sienna was cast in the role of Katya, the soap actress. While Pierre tries desperately hard to undermine Katya's career and beauty, she slowly unravels his experiences as a war correspondent in Bosnia during the 1990s.

Directed by Steve Buscemi (who also plays the part of Pierre), *Interview* was a low-budget production, with a cost of just £800,000. Subsequently, the crew had to be resourceful and cut corners wherever possible. Steve Buscemi decorated the set with paintings borrowed from several artist friends and photographs taken by his wife. Rather than re-shoot the same scene from several angles, the cameramen also filmed in real time. Sienna loved the natural fluidity of filming in this way. She described the experience as more like being on a stage than a movie set. 'I struggle as an actor with the continuity side of things,' she complained. 'You have to do a wide shot, a master, close-ups. You try to re-create what you did already. If you've got three cameras, you never have to worry. They've all got the same take. It gives you freedom.'

Playing a famous actress stalked by the paparazzi struck a resonant chord with Sienna. However, drawing a distance between herself and her fictional character, Sienna chose to play Katya as an extrovert who courts the camera. 'Katya enjoys being famous,' she explains. 'She walks into a restaurant at night with her sunglasses on. There's a side to her that embraces this; it's her public persona. I definitely play her like that, but I don't personally feel that way. With actors there is media interest, but I just wish it wasn't so to the degree I've been subjected to in the past. I reached the stage, especially in England, where things spiral out of control, in which I realised I'm fighting a losing battle and can't win.'

Regardless of complications in her private life, Sienna was delighted to be taking part in the film. Unfortunately, not everyone felt the same way. In 2004, Theo van Gogh produced a ten-minute film, *Submission*, depicting four abused and partially naked Muslim women. The film sparked a huge controversy, which ultimately resulted in Van Gogh's murder a few weeks later. A legacy of conflict still surrounded his works. When Steve Buscemi chose to remake *Interview*, he was prepared for some retaliation from the Muslim community. True enough, one morning Sienna awoke to find several death threats on her doorstep. Islamic extremists threatened the actress with violence if she continued to work on the film. As she read over the threats, her heart sank. At first she couldn't believe they were real. Nothing like this had ever happened to her before. Immediately, she picked up the phone and rang Steve. 'Don't worry, I've had them as well,' he reassured her.

After a lengthy discussion, Sienna felt a lot more at ease. Her fear ebbed away and in its place came defiance. She would not be bullied into giving up on a project she believed in. She had to carry on. She owed it both to the crew and to herself. 'The film hasn't got anything to do with Islam, but, because it's being made as a tribute to Theo, the Islamic fundamentalists have hit the roof,' reported a source. 'Sienna refuses to give into these threats. The people behind them represent everything she abhors.'

A bodyguard was hired to look after Sienna. 'We'll ensure that Sienna and her co-star Steve Buscemi get protection,' told an official from the film set.

By now, Hollywood was awash with word on Sienna Miller. No longer just the pretty appendage to Jude Law, she was starting to make a name in her own right. That said, with several films still in production, the jury remained 'out' on her credentials as a bona-fide actress. The response to *Casanova* had been lukewarm. Now Sienna had an opportunity to prove herself. Admirers were willing the ambitious actress to achieve, while critics were simply waiting to bring her down. From now on, Sienna would need to tread carefully.

If Sienna was honest with herself, she loved being in America. In a land of celebrities, the press had their pick of candidates to follow. Sienna was just one of many and was consequently less harangued than she had been in the UK. She also relished the opportunity to acquaint herself with a whole new set of friends. Ending her relationship with Jude had been a big turning point. She was desperate for a new start and a new lifestyle. A relative newcomer to Hollywood, she was still quite overwhelmed by all the glitz and glamour.

Attending the Academy Awards was a huge highlight of Sienna's calendar. Sat in her room at the Chateau Marmont Hotel, Sienna fondly recalled her first visit to the Awards with her ex-boyfriend Daniel. Back then, she had been a relative nobody, able to sneak around the party, gossiping and giggling about other celebrities. On another occasion, she'd attended the ceremony with Jude. At that point in her life she'd have been a fine candidate for best supporting girlfriend. Now she was alone. For a moment she felt sad. Wistfully, she imagined how differently her life might have turned out had Jude managed to remain faithful.

'Briiiiing!' roared her mobile phone. She sat up suddenly with a jolt. It was her friend Keira Knightley. Keira had been nominated for an Oscar and was experiencing a bout of pre-award nerves. The UK press had glorified the anxious *Pride and Prejudice* star as the UK big hope in America. She'd been put under an unbearable amount of pressure to do her nation proud. 'You get trotted out like Britain's prize poodle and they give you marks out of ten for what you are wearing and what your jewels are like. It's a bit scary,' she complained. The 20-year-old was out enjoying dinner at The Ivy (LA), when hordes of fans and photographers descended on the restaurant. Struggling to cope with the furore around her, Keira called on Sienna in a fit of panic. Sienna suggested her friend come over to the Chateau Marmont straight away. After a drink and a friendly pep talk, she managed to calm the young star down.

Unfortunately, later that night at the *Vanity Fair* Oscars after-party, Sienna would receive some unwanted attention of her own. Refusing to give rise to any further rumours about her love life, Sienna asked her best pal Tara Summers to be her date for the night. If there was one thing the break-up with Jude had taught Sienna, it was to stick closely to her friends. Sienna and Tara were determined to have a laugh from the outset. While staid and serious men in suits spoke in hushed conversation, Sienna and her pal were caught cavorting wildly with cocktails in hand. By all accounts, they were the life and soul of the party. Photographs of their antics would later be published as part of an Oscars feature in *Vanity Fair*. In one shot, Tara appeared to be nibbling her pal's toes, while in another Sienna was seen hitching up her dress and waving a bare leg at the camera.

Sienna and Tara were in hysterics when they saw the final pictures. Both girls agreed they'd had a great night. However, judging by the newspaper reports that followed, not everyone shared in Sienna's idea of fun. One party guest described the playful actress as 'loud' and 'childish'. Another warned that her antics had placed a serious question mark over her fledgling Hollywood career. 'It's one thing to be gossiped about, but it's quite another to have pictures of yourself in that kind of clinch plastered all over a magazine,' they fumed to the *Mail on Sunday*. 'Hollywood is notoriously straight-laced when it comes to the behaviour of a young star. This is an industry town. Actresses who expect to be taken seriously simply don't get drunk and behave like this in public.' It appeared Sienna was the talk of Tinseltown – for all the wrong reasons.

A spokeswoman for Sienna denied any suggestion that Sienna's behaviour had damaged her career. 'They [Tara and Sienna] have just wrapped a film together and they were just sitting next to each other at a party. Nothing more than that. We've had no complaints.'

In other reports of the time, it was claimed that Sienna's pals were becoming increasing concerned about her hectic party lifestyle. One story even had Sienna flirting outrageously with Sean Penn in a bar. 'She's partying hard, some of us would say too hard. We sat her down and told her she needed to count to ten and cool it,' said a pal. But they were quick to defend Sienna's behaviour as the inevitable fallout of a broken heart. 'People need to remember she's still very young and impressionable. And the fall-out from Jude has left her very bruised.'

Within a matter of weeks, Sienna's fledgling friendship with Keira Knightly also appeared to be in trouble. If reports were to be believed, Sienna had apparently made a play for Keira's ex-boyfriend, Irish model Jamie Dornan. Jamie and Sienna were reportedly seen together at the Electric bar in London after becoming neighbours in Notting Hill. Onlookers reported the pair were 'flirting outrageously'. A friend of Keira's claimed the young actress was furious. 'Keira still holds a flame for Jamie… There is every chance that he and Keira might one day get back together, so she will be spitting feathers that Sienna is trying to get her mitts on him.' However, another report suggested Keira had phoned Sienna to warn her of Jamie's insecurities. Allegedly, Keira and Jamie split up when the model was unable to cope with her fame. However, it wasn't long before Jamie was linked with other eligible females, such as Kate Moss.

Nevertheless, Sienna's family decided it was time to intervene. While no one doubted Sienna had behaved anything but respectably at the bash, it was obvious that her delicate reputation was now under fire. Sienna's older sister Savannah decided to take matters into her own hands. She hated all the machinations of the media and had never really understood why Sienna allowed herself to be played by such a cruel and intrusive crowd. She was also fiercely protective of her younger sibling and she perhaps felt a responsibility to safeguard her interests. In stark contrast to her sister, Savannah lived a life of relative peace and calm in a cottage by the sea in Cornwall. She called Sienna and suggested she come and visit for a few days. The pair had hardly spent any time together in the previous few months – Sienna was forever jetting off to foreign climes for yet another film shoot. While Savannah was pleased to see her sister's career progress, she also recognised a need to apply the brakes every now and then. 'Savannah is laid-back and not into any trendy London scene. She feels her sister has been caught up in a whirlwind of media attention ever since she and Jude Law broke up,' claimed a source.

The last time the two sisters had the opportunity to spend any quality time together was at Christmas when, along with their mum Jo, they'd taken a holiday in Mexico. As far as Savannah was concerned, a visit to the country was well overdue. In need of a rest, Sienna agreed to take her sister up on the offer. The pair took long walks together, discussing events of the previous 12 months.

Savannah even managed to persuade her sister to switch off her mobile phone. She needed some time away from Jude and all her other acting pals. In the evenings, the sisters enjoyed hearty meals at the local pub or stayed in and cooked together. It was exactly the break Sienna needed to recharge her batteries.

Although Sienna was struggling to rebuild her identity, she was certainly making progress. Closing a chapter on her old life wasn't easy. Part of the process had been to change her dress sense. Sienna had fought desperately hard to shake off her 'boho-chic' fashion tag. Some of her fashion statements had been extreme, to say the least. On one occasion, she even went out in New York dressed in a designer swimsuit and trilby hat. Not all the magazine fashion editors were suitably impressed. As a mark of rebellion, Sienna had also opted for a tattoo. She chose to have three tiny blue stars inked on her shoulder.

Despite the odd fashion faux-pas, Sienna was still regarded as a style icon, and it wasn't long before a fashion house approached the actress about collaborating on a new line of clothing. Pepe Jeans offered her a multimillion-pound deal to produce her own unique line of jeans and she signed on the dotted line immediately. Sienna would design a range of jeans to suit all sizes, modelling several of the pairs herself.

The reluctant style siren was over the moon. Her contract did, however, include a clause preventing her from wearing anyone else's jeans. Magazines set to work, hunting for pictures of Sienna in rival lines. They struck gold with a picture of Sienna in a pair of LoFLi jeans. Gleefully, they claimed Sienna had broken her contract, but fortunately for Sienna the picture turned out to be an old one. Satisfied their client had not been in the wrong, Pepe chose not to tear up their contract.

A few weeks later, Sienna was invited to host a huge party in New York celebrating British style. The AngloMania Ball was a lavish affair and was an opening event for a new exhibition celebrating British design at New York's Metropolitan Museum of Art. The star-studded party featured several different themed rooms, including a Hunt Ball and a Gentlemen's Club. Celebrities in attendance included Liz Hurley, Kate Moss and Naomi Campbell. Representing the US were Jennifer Lopez, Sarah Jessica Parker and Richard Gere. Sienna picked out a gold sequinned mini-dress by Burberry for the event. She teamed it up with opaque black stockings, with her hair tied back in a simple ponytail. Kate Moss chose to wear a sharp, fitted black jacket and skin-tight satin trousers, her hair pulled back elegantly. Naomi Campbell, meanwhile, went for a pale gold gown. Sienna was delighted to be taking part in the event. Despite her issue with the UK press, she was extremely proud to be British.

But Sienna's new forays into fashion didn't end with clothes. According to tabloid reports, Sienna had found herself a new love interest – 31-year-old Argentinean hotel owner and DKNY model Nico (Nicholas) Malleville.

The pair originally met while working on a shoot together for Burberry with world-famous photographer Mario Testino. Laughing and joking in between shots, they instantly hit it off and decided to stay in contact. But it was only much later that romance finally blossomed.

Eager to spend some time with Sienna, Nico invited her to join him at the exclusive Mayan Riviera resort in Mexico. The pair checked into the Coqui Coqui Spa on Tulum beach, owned by Nico. 'The spa was the perfect retreat for them,' an insider reported. 'It's like your own personal tropical hideaway, so it was ideal for Sienna and Nico to get to know each other better away from prying eyes.' According to reports, Sienna and Nico enjoyed several romantic candlelit dinners on the beach and tried several pampering spa treatments. They then set off to visit the Mayan ruins and the Aktun Ha caves. Ever since her six-month stint in Central America as a teenager, Sienna had always loved travelling.

The reports didn't end there. Sienna and Nico were also spotted dining out in Manhattan. When Sienna flew back to London, her model man quickly followed. He allegedly invited Sienna to a friend's wedding, using it as an opportunity to show her off to his circle. 'At first, she was a little wary of the wedding invite, as it would mean meeting all his close friends and formalising things between them, but she soon gave in,' claimed an insider.

By this point, Nico was already besotted by the emotionally troubled star. When he was required to attend a modelling shoot in Milan for the shoemaker Tod's, he begged Sienna to join him. According to reports, Sienna was desperate to accompany him but couldn't juggle her schedule. She did, however, invite him to spend a few days with her in London afterwards.

Unfortunately for Nico, however, it wasn't long before Jude reappeared in the picture. Uncertain about her future, Sienna invited her estranged lover to join her on set in New York. Jude dropped everything to join her and flew out immediately. Their meeting went well and it looked as if, once again, a reconciliation was on the cards. 'Since the split, they've both realised they once had something great,' said a close pal.

A few weeks later, Jude invited Sienna to spend some time with him in LA. She duly took him up on the offer. The actor had hired a house in Topanga Canyon for himself and his children and Sienna was delighted by the opportunity to spend time with her surrogate family. She and Jude were also trying desperately hard to rebuild their friendship. When their relationship had ended so abruptly, Sienna had lost not only her lover but also her best mate. His exit left a gaping void in her life. She'd tried desperately hard to fill that gap with work, but it soon became obvious she was lonely.

Pictures of the pair climbing into a car together seemed to confirm their troubled relationship was back on again. Several weeks later, there were more sightings of the twosome in Malibu and Santa Monica. Careful to protect their privacy, the couple went to great measures not to be seen together. It was hard enough trying to patch up their differences in private, let alone in front of an audience. While out in LA, they decided to go on a family outing to the cinema to see a screening of *Ice Age 2*. However, on leaving the auditorium, they were ambushed by several photographers. They quickly left, Sienna in the car and Jude taking a cab.

It was a routine that had become all too familiar in the previous 12 months. Jude had already had a go at a photographer for taking pictures of his children. When the paparazzi chose to rudely interrupt the couple's family outing, a friendly local police escort intervened and drove them to the trendy Urth Café restaurant, where they grabbed some takeaway food.

The couple were sighted again at Hollywood hot-spot Shag. This time, they were in the company of young Disney Queen-turned-Hollywood starlet Lindsay Lohan. As a gesture to her newfound friends, Lindsay even offered to act as a decoy, leaving the club first so as to absorb a frenzy of flash bulbs from photographers waiting outside. Much to Nico's dismay, Sienna had decided to give Jude another chance. He took time out to mend his broken heart by attending the Cannes Film Festival with Paris Hilton, Stavros Niarchos and rising fashion star Julia Restoin. When quizzed by journalists about his supposed relationship with Sienna, he snapped, 'Whatever… Sienna can be like a dog that's chasing its own tail.'

Nico wasn't the only one aggrieved by the couple's reconciliation. Furious at Jude's stupidity, Sadie Frost lashed out at her ex-husband. She and Jude had become extremely close over the previous few months and she was determined to have her say. She allegedly told her ex-husband in an email that Sienna would never make him happy. 'Sadie said he was mad to go back to Sienna. She said he really changes when he is with her, he becomes stressed and emotionally all over the place.' Incensed by her reaction, Jude showed the email to Sienna. She apparently sent an email back, accusing Sadie of being jealous and unable to accept that Jude had moved on. Sadie apparently responded with an angry phone call to Jude: 'I'm not going to be there to nurse your wounds when she drives you mad – and it will happen.'

And it did happen. Now on a roll with movie offers, Sienna set to work on her next feature, *Camille*. Another independent, the film was pitched as a twisted honeymoon road trip about a young couple on their way to Niagara Falls. A petty thief marries his parole officer's niece, hoping he can use the honeymoon to escape to Canada. Sienna was cast in the role of Camille, a sweet innocent who truly believes Niagara Falls will change her new husband for the better.

Most of the film was shot on location in Canada. Still in the process of rebuilding her relationship with Jude, Sienna was keen he should come and join her on location. According to newspaper reports, however, Jude had other ideas. He preferred to stay at home and spend time with his children. Jude flew out to visit Sienna in a bid to patch up their differences. (He was currently filming *My Blueberry Nights* in New York with Rachel Weisz and Natalie Portman.) According to witnesses, Jude looked bored and miserable. In one instance he even stormed off, leaving Sienna in tears. She apparently fumed at his 'lack of kindness and respect'.

Friends reported Jude was fed up with his on/off girlfriend's constant demands and jealous behaviour. Some claimed Sienna had issued Jude with a set of intolerable demands. He was to call her every two hours and report back his every move.

After several rows, the report claimed Jude had called for a trial separation. Leaving Sienna alone in Toronto, he took his children for a family holiday at his parents' house in France. 'He adores his kids and has always juggled his relationship with her but it seems Sienna wants to have her cake and eat it,' one source alleged. Friends of the couple feared their relationship could be over for good. 'Jude has got to see the light!' fumed one pal. 'We are all sick of him being made a mug. They have to stay apart for their sanity.'

The papers wasted no time in linking Sienna with her new leading man, *Spider-Man* star James Franco, who had been cast as Sienna's love interest in *Camille*. Now something of an expert, Sienna was no longer afraid of filming love scenes. Given that her co-stars were usually easy on the eye, it was never really a problem! In one scene, she and James were required to roll around in the hay kissing. Sienna was wearing a wedding dress while James was topless. After filming had stopped, Sienna cheekily laid her hand on James's groin. 'Oh my God, did I just touch you, Franco?' she joked in front of the crew. 'I've just touched Franco's manhood. Yes, I did, I just touched you!'

After filming had wrapped, the cast all went out for dinner. According to one eyewitness, Sienna and Franco held hands under the table. 'We are holding hands. Naughty. But there is no need to blush now, is there, Franco?' winked Sienna in jest. The pair had quickly become good friends and loved to flirt on set. A romantic tryst seemed inevitable. After all, Sienna did have a habit of falling for her leading men. Just like Hayden, James had become a shoulder to cry on. Onlookers reported that he was full of praise for Sienna and was helping to boost her deflated ego. 'He showers her with praise and attention, which Sienna loves,' said one source. 'He's always running around the set in front of Sienna, laughing and fooling around. She watches him all the time with a big smile on her face.'

On set the two actors were described as inseparable. They would practise lines together, smoke cigarettes and chat intimately. But rumours about the pair spread like wildfire after filming a dream sequence in Niagara Falls. Wearing a wedding dress and riding a blue horse, Sienna sauntered into camera shot. Seconds later James jumped on to the horse and grabbed her in a passionate embrace. 'Cut!' screamed the director, but James refused to let go. Sienna giggled and stroked his hair. Whether it was for the benefit of the cameras or not, Sienna and James definitely shared a magical chemistry.

Off set, their friendship blossomed further. 'Do you fancy checking the Wilco concert at Massey Hall tonight?' James asked his co-star.

'Sure,' she said, smiling.

Dressed in a stripy grey shirt, black hat and black trousers, Sienna set out for the evening. During the show, the pair both nattered constantly. Afterwards, Sienna entertained James by dancing on the pavement. James erupted into fits of laughter. The pair then headed to Chinatown for a late dinner, stepping out for the occasional cigarette. They then carried on at the Brant House nightclub, where they partied until 1.30am.

The following night, the pair attended a screening of *Pirates of the Caribbean: Dead Man's Chest*. According to one witness, James caressed Sienna's face and even gave her a kiss. After leaving the movie, they both went to buy some books. Finally, they popped into a pub to catch some of the World Cup before returning to their hotel rooms.

Even Sienna's mum Jo was fond of James. Jo had flown out to visit Sienna on set and was instantly introduced to her daughter's new best buddy. The three decided to hit the town with a visit to the Fallsview Casino and Resort in Niagara Falls. Bizarrely, Sienna and Jo were dressed in matching green outfits with pink cowboy hats.

But, once again, all was not as it seemed. Days after photographs of James and Sienna were published, Sienna's representative Ciara Parkes spoke out against the rumours. She claimed the intimate pictures had been taken during filming in the presence of a thousand cast and crew members. 'It was a sad scene, the last scene of the movie. They are just joking about during takes,' she claimed.

Friends of Sienna also confirmed she and Jude were still together. 'Sienna and Jude are still very much an item. Just because they are working in different locations doesn't mean they've split up. She and James are friends and even actors are entitled to have friends,' they told America's *People* magazine.

Whether anyone believed the stories or not, they still kept coming in thick and fast. The more Sienna resisted the press, the more they persisted in printing rumours. Clouds of uncertainty and doubt swathed the star's love life, but for the purposes of public interest that's exactly how she liked it. So, for the time being, the Sienna and Jude saga would continue.

Right now, Sienna was too busy to let it bother her. She had several new film projects on the horizon. She was also in the process of filming the new Matthew Vaughn film *Stardust*. A fantastical fairytale, *Stardust* told the story of a young man who makes a promise to his beloved that he'll retrieve a fallen star by venturing into a magical realm. Sienna was also in talks to star as the lead in *The Mysteries of Pittsburgh*, based on Michael Chabon's debut novel. For the foreseeable future, Sienna was very much occupied. It was more than likely that her love life would have to take a back seat...

Over the previous few years, Sienna had changed dramatically. Once naive, innocent and eager to please, she had subsequently become hardened to the pressures of fame. There had been a time when she would quite happily talk about her personal life. These days, she refused to let out even so much as a whisper. Her personal life had crumbled in front of the cameras; every argument, every tear had been detailed in the press. In the previous 12 months, Sienna had lost a lot more than Jude – she'd also lost her privacy and on several occasions her dignity. Over time she'd struggled to regain those and she wasn't about to let them go again without putting up a fight.

Looking back over her life, Sienna reflected on the irony of her situation. For the most part she'd been fortunate. Her childhood was filled with only happy memories. Perhaps it was inevitable that her luck would run out soon. But, rather than get depressed, Sienna was determined to remain positive. Once, Jude Law had been her entire life. That was no longer the case – and it wasn't a bad thing! Able to stand on her own two feet, Sienna realised she didn't need a man to complement her life. All she required was already in her grasp. No longer the girl, the girlfriend or a pretty magazine-cover girl, Sienna Miller had forged her own identity. She was now a force to be reckoned with.

As a little girl, Sienna had dreamed of performing on the stage and entertaining audiences with her talent. Her success was testimony to the fact that dreams do sometimes come true. A reluctant celebrity, she'd unfortunately found fame before she'd been given time to earn respect. Now all of that was changing. Years ago, Sienna's mum had presented her with a CD of music from the *The Nutcracker Suite*. It had, after all, been the soundtrack to her birth. Whenever she felt low, Sienna would close her eyes and listen to the music. She was quickly reminded of why she'd chosen to take this precipitous career path in the first place. Whatever the pressures, it was worth it. Sienna Miller was already in full flight and no one could stand in her way.

Let the sugar plum fairy dance on.